A Note on the Authors

Judy Reith and Adrian Reith are professional coaches and writers. They have been married for over thirty years and have three adult children. They are definitely in Act 3. They work year-round with individuals and groups to create lasting, profound change in life at all stages and particularly in Act 3, using the methods explained in this book. Together they have run multiple *Guardian* Masterclasses, corporate and community seminars and weekend workshops.

Also available by Judy Reith

7 Secrets of Raising Girls Every Parent Must Know
Be a Great Mum
Transform Living with Teenagers

ACT 3

THE ART OF GROWING OLDER

JUDY
REITH

ADRIAN
REITH

unbound

First published in 2020

Unbound
6th Floor Mutual House, 70 Conduit Street, London WIS 2GF

www.unbound.com

Text Design by Ellipsis, Glasgow

A CIP record for this book is available from the British Library

ISBN 978-1-78352-699-4 (paperback)
ISBN 978-1-78352-702-1 (ebook)

Printed and bound in Great Britain by Clays Ltd, Elcograf S.p.A.

For Rosie, Tilly, Phoebe and Nick — because you will be choosing our care home

With special thanks to Professor Richard Vincent
for the chapter on health, and grateful thanks also to
Michael Leunig for his cartoons

Contents

Chapter One: How to Live the Life You Never Had   1

Chapter Two: Begin with the End in Mind   23

Chapter Three: Get Back to Your Roots   29

   1   Attitude   31

   2   Purpose   40

   3   Values   54

   4   Key Relationships   64

Chapter Four: Health and The Science of Growing

   Older, written by Professor Richard Vincent   89

Chapter Five: The Branches of the Tree   115

   1   Work   117

   2   Play   134

   3   Home   146

   4   Friends   159

   5   Money   169

   6   World   179

   7   Your Special Branch   193

Chapter Six: What Helps the Tree   199

Chapter Seven: What Hurts the Tree, Fear and Loss   207

Chapter Eight: Accept Transition   227

Chapter Nine: Act 4 – The Art of Dying   237

Chapter Ten: The End – Or Is It the Beginning?   267

Resources   271

Notes   279

Credits   287

More about the Authors   291

Index   293

Supporters   301

Chapter One

How to Live the Life You Never Had

You cannot go back and change the beginning, but you can start where you are and change the ending.
– James R. Sherman, *Rejection*[1]

You are making history. Something strange has happened to the baby-boom generation and those who came after – our picture of old people no longer fits. Our idea of retirement has retired. We're undergoing a major awakening of what's possible in our 50s, 60s, 70s and beyond.

- A woman we know has had her first baby – she's 51.
- Idols from our youth are active and frighteningly fit. Sit down, Mick Jagger.
- 70- and 80-year-olds are everywhere cycling, in Lycra. With straight faces.

Something's changed. Life has an extra act.

We call it Act 3.

Act 3 is the period from around 50 to 75+ that used to be called retirement. It's now a massive opportunity to enjoy better health and fulfil higher expectations for many more years. No previous generation has had this opportunity.

We, your authors, are in Act 3 ourselves, and in recent years, our eyes and ears have been alerted to those who are up to all sorts. They are making their Act 3 the time when they use their imagination, their strengths and their hard-won wisdom to create a new life full of adventure, meaning and fulfillment – not regrets. It seems there is an art to this, some sort of insider knowledge and certain secrets that need sharing. Some people have really turned on the lights in their twilight years and they have inspired us. We've interviewed many people for this book from many backgrounds – they've been generous in sharing their Act 3 adventures. Some contributors have been given a pseudonym to protect their privacy; others were happy to share their stories more openly.

These stories, along with our coaching experience, are given here to inspire you to create and live your own Act 3 years so you spring out of bed in the morning, with a To Do list that meets your ambitions, your values, not somebody else's.

For some, that might mean travel, for others volunteering or spending time with grandchildren. Or adopting children, as we shall see. It could mean starting a business or a charity. Is it time to write that book, take up painting or learn a new language? Maybe you have always wanted to dance or play an instrument or sail to New Zealand. It's not too late. We'll tell you about Cecil who retrained as a dancer and is now on tour, in his late 60s. Or Trish, aged 70, who has found meaning and purpose in starting an online make-up range for older women. Then there's John, the Cambridge professor of neuroscience now running a café with his son, where milk is poured from a jug John made in his pottery studio.

These people, and many more, are all reinventing the old, tired picture of retirement, and they all share three things in common. As they approached retirement age, they had a great desire to do something *meaningful* and enjoyable in this extra time. They gave themselves *permission* to go after these goals and make them a reality. And they keep in mind there is *increasing risk* in Act 3 that something physical, mental, financial or fatal could scupper dreams and plans — so best get on with it.

Before bits of your body pack up, negativity kicks in, money worries overwhelm you or you breathe your last, what do you want your Act 3 years to be about? That's the only purpose of the book that's in your hands right now.

So, where are you at this stage in your life, and what do we mean by Acts 1, 2, 3 and 4?

Act 1, Act 2, Act 3, Act 4

Act 1 — that's the growing up bit. If it was a season, you'd call it spring. The baby, the child, the teenager and the young adult. Act 1 usually merges into Act 2 when you leave home, but in the current economic climate, that is not as clearly defined as it once was, with many adult children returning to the family nest when jobs, money or romance issues make it the best or only option.

Act 2 — is the summertime stage when you're independent from your parents, and carries on through your 30s, 40s and, for some, into their 50s or beyond. Act 2 is busy. There is money to earn, a career to grow, maybe a life partner or long-term relationships and, for many, raising children, and coping with the decline of their own parents.

Act 3 — and then for many comes retirement, which historically has meant pipe and slippers, decline and death. We could sum-marise Act 3 as a big time of change and increasing loss. From eyesight to waistlines, routines of work and family life, it's all change. And for most women, the physical and emotional upheaval of the menopause will be a major part of their transition into Act 3, and can feel like the end of the world. (It isn't.)

When the state old-age pension was first introduced in 1908, it was for the one in four people who had made it to age 70, and the life expectancy then was an average of nine more years. Therefore, not that long for the state to provide for not that many oldies. A century later, we have millions living longer, creating a huge burden on the state purse.

On the upside, we have this whole new chunk of time to do something with, we are in better health, and with more resources than any previous generation. The autumn of our lives, Act 3.

Act 4 – and after autumn, comes the winter. Our Act 4, when we can be as helpless as a baby, but with the mind of a sage, sitting in a care home with a TV on at full volume. But we're not there yet.

We're interested in Act 3, because this is an exciting time and full of potential.

Moving from Act 2 to Act 3 Can Get Eggy

In the same way, the Act 2 experiences you've had – to leave home, maybe more education, to stand on your own feet, to make a career, to earn some money, perhaps make a relationship, make a home, maybe create a family, take care of health and responsibilities – can be so draining that it results in scrambled-egg brain at the beginning of Act 3. Maybe you forgot what you came for. Is this it? Who am I now? Who do I want to be? Where am I headed?

Scrambled-egg brain: At the end of a long day cycling Land's End to John o'Groat's (870 miles from the bottom of England to the very top of Scotland), my cycle partner Kip and I crawled off our bicycles after 100 hilly, wet, windy miles. Such had been the power drain on our bodies we could barely form thoughts, let alone speak. We were in survival mode. Kip, who was celebrating his 60th, would just say, 'Scrambled egg'. It summed up our inability to think straight.

Having had a shower and supper, the scrambled-egg-brain effect wore off and we were able to make simple decisions again. We'd made the transition.

- Robbie

We think understanding transition is important. It feeds your tree. The tree we are talking about is our unique model to help you create your Act 3. More on the tree soon. You'll find 7 steps that help with transition in the chapter 'The Branches of the Tree'.

My husband retires in 2 weeks.
I'm absolutely dreading it. He has no idea what
he'll do all day.
– corporate lawyer married to corporate lawyer

Relax. This is entirely normal. Lots of people get major egg over themselves without meaning to because they've been so committed to the duties of Act 2, career, family, home. Things get confusing for the best reasons.

Unless, of course, you have a plan. Some people are raring to go . . .

Midlife, not death

The other important truth about mid to later life and the retirement years is facing change and loss. We'll dig into this in more detail, but if you only read this far, part of why we wanted to write this book is to offer an alternative to the destructiveness of midlife crisis behaviour that comes from difficulties around ageing and loss. We have seen too many relationships crash, money spent on stuff that promises to make your life better or addictions dominating your time. The midlife crisis destroys lives and wastes potential. Let's not go there, it's not inevitable.

> I used to find map reading and navigating easy, I was good at it too. But the other day, I got us lost driving to a party, a 30-minute delay which really upset me. I realised it wasn't just being late, it was being faced with getting older . . . losing my map-reading skills.
>
> – Andy, 61

Act 3: The Art of Growing Older could be many books – it's a massive subject. Our goal in writing it has always been to aim for a book that is useful, loved and shared by the reader. We had those words on a Post-it by our computers.

We have curated the parts of Act 3 that we see counting the most. It's written in a workbook style to help you create a much better version of your life at this stage, whether you're ignoring it, in it or almost out the other side.

What you'll get in this book

- How to re-imagine what's possible for you in all the important areas of your life and what your purpose is, in Act 3. We'll give you examples, and a structure to think about values, work, play, home, relationships, you and your interests.
- How to establish achievable goals that satisfy, instead of feeling cheated by life.
- Tips, hints and suggestions to reflect and help you get there. Plus references to further reading and online support.

Write your Act 3 story alongside this book

Part of the process of making a better future for yourself is found in thinking, reflecting and dreaming it into life. This is best done by writing or drawing your notes, your ideas, and your dreams and plans. Please find yourself a lovely notebook to use as a journal as you read the book.

Questions are asked throughout which we hope you'll answer in your journal – you might do these exercises as you read or you might choose to return to them later. It's up to you to decide how best to use your journal.

Be responsible for your own learning. Work at your own pace. Write what you actually feel. Not what you *think* you should feel, or think, or do. Even better, we find it helps to share thoughts and plans you develop from using this book with a partner or a close friend – if and when you are ready.

This is your book, use it however you like. You'll get further faster if you break your own rules. Write what you shouldn't write. Draw what you've never drawn.

Once you have your journal, describe or draw on the first page what you want to gain from reading *Act 3: The Art of Growing Older*.

Language

For clarity we use 'we' when we are referring to ourselves, the authors, and 'you' when we are referring to you, the reader who wants a great Act 3 whatever your circumstances. Any other language we use is intended to make this a clear read, not to be confusing, judgemental or hurtful. Names have been changed where requested to protect the guilty.

Health Warning

We will not:
- Advise you when to retire
- Give you financial advice
- Tell you about pension plans
- Recommend property sales or purchases
- Recommend 'anti-ageing' products
- Recommend a diet
- Shape your exercise regime
- Nag you about your alcohol, drug, smoking or shopping addictions
- Transform your friends and relations
- Judge you

We will:
- Help you feel positive about getting older
- Help you feel quiet, calm and focused
- Reduce your worries
- Help you feel much clearer, less bewildered

- Help you find your own mind to make better decisions about the above
- Help you understand why you're making those decisions
- Help you make your loved ones feel reassured about your ageing years
- Help you have more fun
- Help you have more energy
- Help you get what you really, really want . . .

Real thinking is hard work

The best artists, writers, business people, organisations; the best people in healthcare, the military, science, sports – top people in every walk of life – have to *struggle* to think differently about stuff they are familiar with.

It's *hard* to think new thoughts. *Very hard.* Humans normally conserve energy by acting habitually – not really thinking new, challenging thoughts.

Some housekeeping to note

Take care of yourself along the way: This is not a book about learning holiday French. It will ask the deepest part of your heart and mind to think long and hard about yourself now, and in the future. Sometimes that can hurt. Where you see the 'Take Care' cross, that alerts you to the content and the questions being particularly significant. You are probably better off sitting somewhere quiet for those bits.

TAKE

CARE

Speak out: Say things out loud to yourself. Something changes when you speak thoughts and feelings out loud. You may think this is crazy – it helps clarify what you think and feel about important stuff.

Where are you starting from?: We don't know what you already know about the art of getting older. There are plenty of resources out there on the science of ageing, but this book is more about tapping into the art, the secrets or the knack that some people seem to have that is giving them a really good Act 3.

You'll probably know more than you think, and our intention is to add to your wisdom. Some of what we say could be blindingly obvious. Some of what we say you might not like. Sorry.

Creation: Creating a good Act 3 starts with the imagination. Everyone has one. Children have no problem imagining all kinds of things and asking limitless questions. One of ours asked, 'Do the stars have feelings?' As we move through the relentless stage of Act 2, running our lives, building our home, work and family, our imagination can sometimes wither. There's just so much to DO. But Act 3 is often characterised by more time and possibility; it's a great time to dust off your imagination, and let it run riot, as if you were a kid again.

Every act of creation is first
an act of destruction.[2]

Destruction disclaimer: To create a good new future, you will need to destroy some things. This is normal and right. However, the authors cannot accept responsibility for decisions you make as a result of reading this book. If your partner leaves you, or you leave them ... we hope you'll live with the new reality in a positive way.

How to use this book

We'll give you the scaffolding you need to get the best out of the book.

Let it go. Let it out.
Let it all unravel.
Let it free and it can be
A path on which to travel.

When people wrestle with important stuff, they find it difficult to know where to start to unravel their mental spaghetti. Our method will make it much easier, and very practical.

> We cannot solve our problems with the same
> thinking we used when we created them.[3]

Cut the crap, time is short

We'll help you to imagine, design, create and enjoy your Act 3. After which you'll be thinking and acting differently instead of fumbling around wasting time.

This book is designed to help you increase self-awareness and self-control, and to engage in planning that will enable you to make more satisfying choices about your future.

> *A day is over and so much of it was wasted on things that meant too little to you, duties and meetings from which your heart was absent. Months and years pass and you fumble on, still incapable of finding a foothold on the path of time you walk.*
>
> *A large proportion of your activity distracts you from remembering that you are a guest of the universe, to whom one life has been given. You mistake the insistent pressure of daily demands for reality and your more delicate and intuitive nature wilts. When you wake from your obsessions, you feel cheated.*
>
> *Your longing is being numbed and your longing becomes merely external. Your way of life has so little to do with what you feel and love in the world. But, because of the many demands on you and responsibilities that you have, you feel helpless to gather your self; you are dragged in so many directions away from true belonging.*
> — *John O'Donohue*, Eternal Echoes[4]

Act and think differently

 People think in mental pictures as much as words, so we'll use images as well as stories to help you make progress. Pay attention to the pictures that come to your own mind — don't be shy of reproducing what's in your head in your journal.

I knew I was in a muddle about the house and our future, and it felt like this growing black cloud over the house.

Abandon pictures and thoughts that don't resonate for you. Seize the ones that have power. Notice the little details that appeal to you, you've noticed them for a reason.

There's no rush

We've put quotes, illustrations and stories to ponder to help you connect with your real self. Make a nice drink. Sit down. Switch your phone off. Stop. Breathe. Listen to yourself. Go at your own pace.

The Act 3 tree

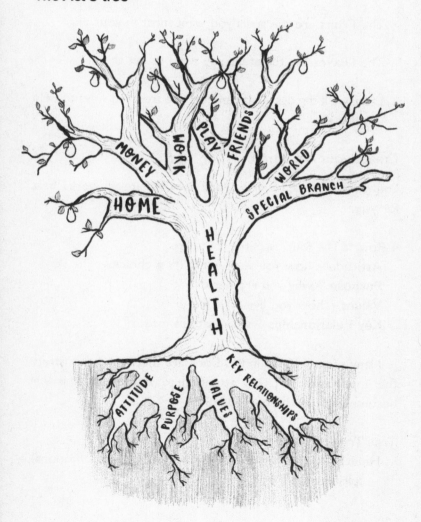

We love trees. We have created the Act 3 tree as a way to focus on all the areas of your life that are most likely to need attention. Some parts of the tree are more important than others – the **4 Roots** come first. They sustain everything.

The **7 Branches** stand for the areas that affect and involve you daily.

The **Fruits** are the goals you want most in your life.

The **Leaves** are the steps you need to get there.

Later we'll discuss what can hurt the tree and ways to help the tree.

Create your Act 3 tree

You can use ours, or draw your own. Whatever works best for you.

4 Roots: The four essential roots are:
Attitude – how you view Act 3. It's a choice.
Purpose – why you are here.
Values – how you live your life.
Key Relationships – who matters most.

Many of the stories in this book are there to demonstrate the importance of paying attention to your roots. This will become clear as the book unfolds.

Tree Trunk:
Health – what's needed for life: physical, mental, emotional, spiritual.

7 Branches: The main areas of our lives that thrive, or don't, in Act 3:

Work – paid or unpaid.

Play – what you do to regenerate.

Home – what kind, and where will it be?

Friends – who is in your life outside of key relationships?

Money – financing your Act 3 and Act 4.

World – external concerns, community, climate change, political and local issues.

Your Special Branch – because there's always something else.

Fruits: These are your fruits/goals at the end of your branches. Your Act 3 goals.

For example, a goal on your 'world' branch might be 'To actively recycle everything I can.' Or on your 'play' branch, 'I will learn a new language before I'm 70.' Or 'home' might be, 'we plan to move to within walking distance of the shops and station in the next 2 years.'

Leaves: Each leaf along the branch represents a step towards your goal. 'Recycling everything I can' could start with 'I'll buy a reusable coffee cup tomorrow.' Or 'I'll look up the French lessons timetable before lunch.' Or 'We'll get our home valued next week.'

How to set goals and take action

Your best Act 3 will come from setting goals that match your values: This will come from clearly knowing what you want. To do that there is a need to be truthful and accepting of your starting point. Admitting you have some work to do.

In our experience people struggle to *see* *clearly* what they *really* want. They also find it difficult to *own up* to what they want. All of this stops people creating excellent goals.

'I don't deserve that' or 'I could never do that' is spoken by a familiar little internal voice that has many opinions about how you should live your life. Is it time to start answering back? Some people give this voice a name, and then tell it to shut up.

> For me it is hard to come up with good goals, because I limit myself so easily. My internal voice says, 'That won't work, that's too difficult, you don't have the skills for that, you tried that before and it didn't work, no one has done that before, things like that don't happen, they won't let you do that . . .'
>
> – Sarah, 58

How do I set goals then?

Your best goals are ones that match your *values* and are not dependent on other people to be reached. You may have heard of S.M.A.R.T. goals. We prefer G.O.A.T.S., we'll explain this shortly.

It's a waste of time setting goals if you don't know what your values are. You'll be in danger of setting the wrong goals, and when you reach wrong goals, you'll be disappointed.

In Act 3, time and energy are even more precious, so spend them well, before it's too late.

Goals via values

Goals that match your values are energising and inspire you to reach them. If your goals are inconsistent with what's fundamentally important to you, you'll find it harder to gather the motivation.

In our coaching work, we encounter many who have gone down the wrong path, wasting precious time and energy chasing goals that weren't right for them. They didn't stop to examine their values first.

We'll say much more about values later – they're a root of your Act 3 tree.

When your values are clear, making decisions becomes easier.

Tricia Cusden started the make-up brand Look Fabulous Forever when she was 65:

I'd wound down all my work commitments that year, and I was literally making an appointment to watch Countdown *in the afternoon which was the only date in my diary! I kept thinking, I don't know what to do, I can't sit here and watch television for the next 30 years. I thought about becoming a magistrate, but I was too old. A Scrabble club, but it was full of nerdy men. I have always loved business, so it was born out of a passion and desire to have an interesting new life where I would meet lots of new people and be challenged and stretched as a person - that was my goal, and happily over the last five years I have had that, and had more fun than at any other time in my life.*

Values are so important, they are one of the four roots of the Act 3 tree. But we're just mapping out the book here and how to use it – like a toolkit for you. Make sure you have read the values root before you actually set any goals.

You need to love your goal in the same way that Tricia loved business, meeting people and being challenged.

Making goals: G.O.A.T.S.: Goals match what matters most to you

G – Genuine: Experience tells us that goals that aren't YOUR genuine goals are not worth bothering with. They need to line up with your values, your purpose and your key relationships.

O – Optimistic: When you have a positive attitude and use optimistic language, you are much more likely to reach that goal.

A – Achievable: No point in setting goals you are going to struggle to reach.

T – Timed: When are you going to do this? Date? Time?

S – Specific: Use clear, simple language so you know exactly where you're heading.

Step 1. Think hard about your goal and check it passes the G.O.A.T.S. test, and is not dependent on other people to reach it.

Step 2. Imagine you have already reached it: What does it feel like to be there? What is going on for you? What can you see, smell and hear? What more could you do?

For example: Diana and Gordon were considering downsizing:

We had been aware for some years that our home was too big and expensive for us to maintain. It is was of huge importance to us to stay close to our community and our friends - they're so great. We simply wouldn't consider moving to a new town, as our existing relationships, transport and what's on offer here are very important to us.

It became clear our goal was to move to a 3-bedroomed modern house, within 2 miles of where we live, by the time we were 65. Writing down all the benefits of reaching this goal and imagining in detail what it would be like to live in the right house to grow old in really helped spur us into action to clear out all the junk, spruce up the paintwork and get the house valued.

Measuring the progress of goals

This is where the leaves on the tree come in. Like steps on a journey, the leaves build your progress along the branch towards your fruit – your goal.

Score the goal out of 10: Create a clear picture of how much work needs doing to reach your goal. What exactly are the steps to get you there, and how will you measure your progress?

So, reaching the goal is 10/10: The next step is to define your end goal sentence using the G.O.A.T.S. method. That will be your 10/10. For example, the goal of the couple wanting to downsize was 'to move to a 3-bedroomed modern house, within 2 miles of where we live, by the time we were 65'. Achieving that was their 10/10.

What is the current score for the goal?: At this point the couple are still in the old family home. They've made no progress towards downsizing, so they score themselves 3/10.

What's the next step?

What's the first step to move that score up? To create the next leaf along the branch? They decided their first step was to clear out the junk. (The next step was to repaint, the one after that, to get the valuations in.)

Creating steps that get results

Steps, like goals, should be expressed as G.O.A.T.S.: For this couple, their G.O.A.T.S. steps looked like this:

G – Genuine: *Much as we love the junk we've collected, it's more important to get rid of it to free up options for the move. (Values, purpose and key relationships aligned.)*

O – Optimistic: *Imagining having cleared the junk, or upcycled it, will give us the energy to get on with the painting. (Pays attention to Attitude.)*

A – Achievable: *We will set aside four weekends to do this.*

T – Timed: *We'll do the diary tonight, and make sure the junk is cleared by Easter.*

S – Specific: *We will make a detailed list tonight of what else we need to do to progress our goal to downsize successfully.*

Get support

Don't feel it's all up to you. Who else needs to know of your plans, and when?

Remind yourself of progress you've made. Rinse and repeat . . .

> *Two years in, we've settled into our new home, and we're astonished how good it's been. It's opened up time and energy to do things we actually like doing and we don't miss the extra bedrooms. Let alone the junk.*
> *- Diana and Gordon*

So we've come to the end of the instructions for how to use the book. Thank you for your patience, and please reread the instructions as you go if you need to. This is about acting differently in Act 3.

> If you do what you've always done, you'll get
> what you've always got.
>
> – Unknown

Chapter Two

Begin with the End in Mind

If I'd known I was going to live this long, I'd have taken better care of myself.
– Eubie Blake, musician, age 96 who thought he was 100

This chapter is about perspective: it starts with the fact of death and the possibility of regret on the deathbed. The intention of the Act 3 book is to live life without regrets.

We'd like you to take a brave leap and imagine your life is ending. Being faced with that takes guts and imagination, but it also sharpens the mind and puts things into perspective. We said earlier you might read some things that make you uncomfortable – some people have said to us, 'Please don't write about death,' but in our view, it's essential to help you create your best Act 3, before Act 4 shuts you down.

Life before death

How do you get to your deathbed without regrets? By being honest with yourself. By understanding yourself. By accepting yourself without judgement. And working on specific things to create a positive, satisfying strategy to *act and think differently*. Before it's too late.

Do this and you'll achieve far more than just avoiding regrets. You will create an Act 3 you're proud of and energised by, with a positive legacy.

What is the wisdom of the dying?

In her book *The Top Five Regrets of the Dying*, Bronnie Ware, an Australian palliative care-worker, gathered thoughts from terminal patients in her care. Below is her summary as featured in the *Guardian*:[1]

1. I wish I'd had the courage to live a life true to my-self, not the life others expected of me

'This was the most common regret of all. When people realise that their life is almost over and look back clearly on it, it is easy to see how many dreams have gone unfulfilled. Most people had not honoured even a half of their dreams and had to die knowing that it was due to choices they had made, or not made. Health brings a freedom very few realise, until they no longer have it.'

2. I wish I hadn't worked so hard

'This came from every male patient that I nursed. They missed their children's youth and their partner's companionship. Women also spoke of this regret, but as most were from an older generation, many of the female patients had not been breadwinners. All of the men I nursed deeply regretted spending so much of their lives on the treadmill of a work existence.'

3. I wish I'd had the courage to express my feelings

'Many people suppressed their feelings in order to keep peace with others. As a result, they settled for a mediocre existence and never became who they were truly capable of becoming. Many developed illnesses relating to the bitterness and resentment they carried as a result.'

4. I wish I'd stayed in touch with my friends

'Often they would not truly realise the full benefits of old friends until their dying weeks and it was not always possible to track them down. Many had become so caught up in their own lives that they had let golden friendships slip by over the years. There were many deep regrets about not giving friendships the time and effort that they deserved. Everyone misses their friends when they are dying.'

5. I wish I had let myself be happier

'This is a surprisingly common one. Many did not realise until the end that happiness is a choice. They had stayed stuck in old patterns and habits. The so-called "comfort" of familiarity overflowed into their emotions, as well as their physical lives. Fear of change had them pretending to others, and to themselves, that they were content, when deep within, they longed to laugh properly and have silliness in their life again.'

Let's begin with the end in mind

Act 3 is the Extra – Bonus – Unexpected – Second Lifetime you've got before decline and death – a rich opportunity to create an entirely different life.

Write your own obituary: We once sat round with a group of friends discussing what our lives might ultimately be all be about. It was suggested we all have a bash at writing our own obituary. Nothing like it for sharpening the mind, and the diary!

We found it very effective to write our own obituaries to help us clarify what we wanted in the future. We know someone who says to himself at bedtime, *'If I died tonight, what would I regret I hadn't done?'* Then he uses that to spur him on to make the next day meaningful and productive.

Beginning with the end in mind is the first thing we're asking you to write in your journal – your obituary. But we're going to give you three different ways to approach this. It's about what will motivate you, and what you have the stomach for. We have found some people want to write their obituary as if it was published in the paper, telling the facts, and the highs and some of the lows of their life. For others, they imagine someone speaking about them at their 85th birthday party, paying tribute to them, especially what they have done in Act 3. But some people prefer to think ten years ahead. To imagine what you would like to be true in the future, can take some guts, so first of all, take care of yourself, choose a time and a place when you are calm, relaxed and feeling able to do this. Don't worry about getting it perfect on the first go. Take a fresh journal page and write or draw as little or as much as you want.

First decide if you are going to write your obituary, your 85th birthday tribute or what you have done in the next ten years. For options two and three, write the future date at the top of the page.

Keep your journal jottings safe; you may want to change it as your life becomes even bigger, fuller and more exciting than you can currently imagine.

Remember to take extra care after you have done this. For some people, this can throw up a lot of feelings, but not all negative ones. It really can help you to gain perspective and reveal what is important to you in Act 3.

Forget regret.
Make a plan instead.

Chapter Three

Get Back to Your Roots

I have learned that as long as I hold fast to my beliefs and values – and follow my own moral compass – then the only expectations I need to live up to are my own.

– Michelle Obama[1]

Let's create your Act 3 tree

There is nowhere better to start than at the roots to create your Act 3 tree. We'll take you through each one, beginning with *Attitude*, then *Purpose*, *Values* and *Key Relationships*.

With attitude, purpose and values, there is some overlap in how you understand them, and how they play out in your life. What we mean by these terms is:

Attitude

The dictionary says: *A settled way of thinking or feeling about something.*

We would add that attitude can change too. 'I used to dread going to the doctor for an annual check-up, but after my friend died at 61, I decided to see it as a bonus of living in a country where this was on offer, and it keeps me in better nick.' It's useful to note here that attitude is closely related to belief which is defined as *An acceptance that something exists or is true, especially one without proof.*

Either way an attitude or belief for our purpose is personal and affects how you behave. 'I can't run ...' is an attitude or belief you hold about yourself. A negative or limiting attitude or belief can be challenged. If an attitude or belief serves you well, hang on to it. 'I believe I can learn a new language in my 70s.'

Purpose

The dictionary says: *The reason for which something is done or created or for which something exists.*

'I want to use my Act 3 to help solve the homeless issue in my town.' Or 'Time stands still when I'm growing vegetables / cycling / hang gliding / public speaking / building sheds / running my business ...'

Values

The dictionary says: *Principles or standards of behaviour; one's judgement of what is important in life.*

We would add they create a moral compass, how you decide what is right and what is wrong. 'I want to be a reliable volunteer at the food bank.'

Key Relationships

Our fourth root is a sensitive one, but we won't fudge it. Loneliness can be a huge issue for many in Act 3, yet if we have at least one relationship that sustains us somewhat or even a great deal in Act 3, we will do much better.

How ever you understand the definitions of the roots, the important thing is to take notice of what's useful to you as you read on.

The order of the tree roots *does* matter as you'll see ...

We start with attitude.

Root 1 - Attitude

Attitude is a small thing
that makes a big difference.

Attitude is like the tiny rudder that turns a huge ship. Our attitude in Act 3 is crucial. It can make the difference between having a productive and rewarding Act 3 when we are – or choose to be – flexible, hopeful and positive. Attitude *is* a choice – and believing that will empower you to reboot your approach to  creating your Act 3 life. Sometimes it's hard to take that on board for yourself – it's easier to spot a poor attitude in other people. It's scary to make changes and you might feel it's inauthentic to just tell yourself to see things differently, as if you'll lose a bit of the real you in the process. We disagree. We think you'll swap the part of you that is holding you back, not doing you any favours, for something much better. Without a healthy and positive attitude, your tree will really struggle. We tend to think it is the most important root, because if you change your attitude, you can do something much more constructive about your purpose, your values and your key relationships, and, of course, your branches.

A bad attitude is like a flat tyre.
You can't move until you change it.

What is attitude?

Attitude is the emotion, belief and behaviours you have towards something. *A position you take up.* It's a choice.

Attitudes are often the result of experience, circumstance or upbringing, and they can have a powerful influence over behaviour, particularly in Act 3 when we're more set in our ways.

We have to say our own attitudes are not perfect. Not by a long way. And this makes it hard to write about because though we believe in honesty, integrity and consistency, it's extremely hard to live with a 100% positive attitude all the time. Our states of mind change. They're affected these days by late nights, too much food and drink, not enough exercise, bad news, menopause surges and, well, all sorts of things.

Good. So that lets us off the hook nicely.

> We are often less kind than we want to be
> because it makes us feel vulnerable.
> – Adam Phillips[2]

Where do attitudes come from?

As we said earlier, every adult human being has an *inner critic* that pipes up in their head – probably for self-protection. Sometimes it's their own voice and sometimes it's the voice of other influential people, like parents or an overbearing teacher.

Tut tut

The inner critic tut tuts at us, tells us off, kills ideas, action, ambitions and joy before they get to develop.

> If you believe you can,
> or believe you can't,
> you are right.
> – Henry Ford[3]

Good news: attitude can be changed, as this legend shows:

An old Cherokee is teaching his grandson about life. 'A fight is going on inside me,' he said to the boy. 'It is a terrible fight and it is between two wolves. One is evil – he is anger, envy, sorrow, regret, greed, arrogance, self-pity, guilt, resentment, inferiority, lies, false pride, superiority and ego.' He continued, 'The other is good – he is joy, peace, love, hope, serenity, humility, kindness, benevolence, empathy, generosity, truth, compassion and faith. The same fight is going on inside you – and inside every other person, too.' The grandson thought about it for a minute and then asked his grandfather, 'Which wolf will win?' The old Cherokee simply replied, 'The one you feed.'

When did you last change your attitude?

Think of a time when you have changed your attitude to something and it really helped. Make a note in your journal.

I thought you'd like to know, after the workshop, I finally deleted from my computer all the negative emails I was holding on to from an ex-girlfriend who'd sent me hate mail. I realised, I no longer want to feed the 'evil' wolf inside me but the 'good' one in the hope of becoming happier, more serene, calmer and a better balanced person in regards to this relationship.

– Peter

Attitude has power

Roger Bamber, a partner in a law firm, was diagnosed with leukaemia, and went with Nicky, his wife, to the local hospital to commence chemotherapy. Talking to the specialist nurse at the outset their first question was, 'What is the most important factor for the best chance of survival?' Without hesitation the nurse said, 'Your attitude.'

(There's more of Roger's story in Chapter Nine where he talks about planning for his death . . .)

> Optimism helps to create and maintain motivation to reach realistic goals. Success is often achieved when an individual believes that they will succeed.

What are beliefs then?

Attitudes and beliefs are very similar. Negative beliefs come from deep down inside us, and sometimes feel so hard-wired we don't realise their power over us and what they stop us doing, and how they rule our behaviour . . .

An attitude is a belief in action. A choice.

A belief (negative or positive) is often expressed as an 'I statement'. For example, negative ones might be:

- *'I'm not a runner'*
- *'I can't do maths'*
- *'I'm not a planner'*
- *'I can't cook'*
- *'I'm not very good with money'*

Negative beliefs limit our interactions with the world. They create destructive generalisations:

- 'Old people have had their day'
- 'Women are bad drivers'
- 'Men can't multitask'

We can be ruled by these attitudes and beliefs, but we can also decide we've had enough of these things that limit us.

> My dad always said, 'Your sisters are musical, but not you.' I'm 57, and a few months ago, after a lifetime of believing I wasn't musical, a friend persuaded me to join a local choir. I was really nervous at first, but hearing on day one from the choir leader, 'All are welcome, everyone can sing,' I gave it a go. Now, I see myself as someone who can sing. In fact, I'm paying for some singing lessons. It's been a liberation.
>
> – Janice

Janice's new belief in her musical ability has brought her confidence to see herself as someone who can question and conquer limiting beliefs. She's now thinking, 'If I can do that, then what else can I do . . .?'

It's only my BODY that's eighty!

– Pip Wilson

Think about the beliefs that you have, and the kind of story they tell about you that perhaps it's time to rewrite.

What are your beliefs?

You need time, space and a comforting peaceful environment to do this exercise. If you prefer, leave it to

TAKE

CARE

the end of the chapter when you can make the right time available.

Write down any negative beliefs you have about yourself that you would like to change – starting with 'I':
- *I believe ...*
- *I am ...*
- *I can't ...*
- *I will always ...*
- *I'll never ...*

Turning round beliefs and attitudes

We pay a huge price to hold on to these beliefs. If you turned them round, so you believed the *opposite*, what would that do for you? Imagine that.

When you're ready, beside each of your beliefs above, write answers to both these questions:

What is it costing you to keep believing this stuff about yourself?

How would your life be different if you believed the opposite was true?

Man often becomes what he believes himself to be. If I keep on saying to myself that I cannot do a certain thing, it is possible that I may end by really becoming incapable of doing it. On the contrary, if I have the belief that I can do it, I shall surely acquire the capacity to do it, even if I may not have it at the beginning.

– Mahatma Gandhi

Labels kill good attitude

Labels are one-word descriptions that reduce potential and affect attitude.

> *Without realising, I had labelled my wife Jane as a non-runner. In 20 years of marriage I'd literally never seen Jane break into a jog. Jane also thought of herself as a non-runner until the day – approaching her 50th birthday – she decided she must do something about her fitness and set out with trainers on, determined to run round the park. She ran for 20 metres then had to walk for 40, all the while thinking, 'Adam will be laughing and saying, "See, you're not a runner!"' Actually, I wasn't laughing. I admired her. Eight years on now aged 58, Jane has completed numerous fun runs, 5ks, and even a 10k – all without walking. Jane has run off her non-runner label.'*
>
> *– Adam*

Labels are for luggage not people.

Unstick the labels

What labels do you carry? It can hurt remembering labels we have been given. Many parents Judy has coached have felt guilty realising they have been labelling their children, as 'the clever one', 'the sporty one' or 'the middle child'.

Write down labels that other people have stuck on you. Even positive labels create a pressure to live up to them.

Then, put a line through the whole lot. Tear the page out if you want. You are far more than labels, which belong on luggage, not you, and especially in your Act 3.

> *My dad always said I was the clever one. I never liked it, and I felt I had to live up to it or he would be disappointed in me. It created tension and arguments with my brother – I think some of that is still hanging around and we're now in our 60s and Dad is long gone.*
>
> *- Stewart*

Speak what you feel aloud

There's a strange truth about attitudes: we've worked with so many people who have thoughts swirling around in their heads like spaghetti, that never get untangled – which is exhausting and frustrating. The tangle starts to get better when we ask them to voice out loud everything on their minds at the moment and write it down. Then we ask them to write down what's going well, even the smallest thing.

Attitudes change after we create positive actions and take the first step.

An attitude of gratitude

UK politician Denis Healey and his wife Edna in retirement would often turn to each other and say, 'AWL', their private code for *Aren't We Lucky*. They found it helpful to have an attitude of gratitude on a daily basis.

Act - to change your attitude

Remind yourself regularly of what is good in the moment, 'Aren't I lucky, I've got a cup of coffee.' It's a mindful practice that keeps our attitude in a positive place. It seems trivial, but in fact the effects over time are profound, *particularly if you speak it out loud.*

> AWL
>
> or
>
> AIL (Aren't I Lucky)

Set a calm, peaceful sound as a reminder on your phone. When it goes off, immediately think of one thing you are grateful for. Say it out loud.

We ourselves pinched AWL from the Healeys some years ago and use it often.

When Act 3 is tough

It's normal for moods to go up and down in Act 3 with more time and space to think, and an awareness of mortality. If you're going through a rough patch, make a list every night before you go to sleep of three things you're grateful for today. If you need it, get professional help.

One-minute summary: Attitude

Your attitude is affected by your beliefs, your inner critic and labels. This prevents you having the life you could in Act 3. To change to a positive attitude, you need to face your inner critic head on. Rewrite your beliefs and destroy sticky labels. Voice out loud what you want to believe about yourself and write it down. Changing your attitude starts with small steps. For example, 'I can't run 5k.' Then write next to it: 'But I can walk 5k and can run for short bursts of that. So I will, Tuesday, at 9 a.m.' Regularly acknowledge what you are grateful for. We are grateful you are reading this book.

> Our greatest freedom is the freedom to choose
> our attitude.

Root 2 – Purpose

Life is never made unbearable by circumstances,
but only by lack of meaning and purpose.
– Viktor Frankl, *Man's Search for Meaning*[4]

Rather like values, purpose is another tricky word that may take a little thinking about to get a handle on, but as holocaust survivor Viktor Frankl found when he was imprisoned in a concentration camp, it can be life-sustaining.

Purpose in a death camp

In his short book *Man's Search for Meaning*, Austrian psychiatrist and holocaust survivor Frankl observes that, as slave-labourer inmates in Auschwitz and Dachau concentration camps, everybody was in the same terrible circumstances. Despite that, a number of prisoners were able to hold on to some sort of *purpose* – enough meaning to sustain themselves and survive. The many who could not locate any purpose gave up and died.

Frankl says humans are primarily driven by a 'striving to find meaning in one's life', and this sense of purpose gives resilience and enables people to overcome painful experiences. In the prison camp the only place to find that meaning was by each individual reaching inside her- or himself, as their external reality was the same for all.

Purpose sustains life

Frankl's experience shows that purpose (or meaning, which we take to be the same thing) sustains a person's life. It keeps you alive. Some would say it feeds your soul.

What could the soul be?

Judy was sitting beside her mum as she died after 9 years of suffering from Alzheimer's. It struck Judy, in the moment of death – something left her mum's body. Words seem a bit useless describing this, but Judy felt she wanted to say it was her mum's soul departing. Judy doesn't understand it. She doesn't know where her mum's soul has gone, but she likes to believe she'll meet her again, somehow, some might say in heaven, but who knows?

When thinking about the soul other words come to mind. For some, they might think in terms of spirit, heart, essence, the universe, force, agency, the self, the why, the real you ... humans have talked about this for ever, and some religious people find it easier. We think it's that hard-to-describe, unique, mysterious-but-important bit of you. The bit that gives you 'both your North Star and your inner compass', as Richard Rohr puts it in *Falling Upward,* a book about how the failings of the first half of our life can bring spiritual growth, purpose and meaning in the second half.

These are ancient and mysterious things to think about, but whatever your beliefs (or none), or understanding about the soul, what we repeatedly see is that for a successful happy life in Act 3, you need a purpose – a sense of who you are and where you are going. A reason to get up every day. It could be to save the world, or it could be to walk the dog. Both give purpose. Both can feed the soul.

On a workshop we ran, some people found it hard to define purpose or to come up with a purpose. Others were very clear on both counts. Either way, we agreed, you may not know yet what your purpose is, but *deciding to look* for your purpose is in itself purposeful.

TAKE
CARE

We have asked you to consider some weighty ideas. It will help you to write your response to this, but make sure you're in the right frame of mind to do so.

Take out your journal and reread what you wrote in your obituary, 85th birthday tribute or ten-year plan.

From this, what would you, or other people say your life was about – its purpose? Anything you want to add, enlarge or take away?

Without a healthy purpose root, it's impossible to support your tree and get what you want out of life.

> The chance to shape one's story is essential to sustaining meaning in life.
> – Atul Gawande, *Being Mortal*[5]

Advertising sells (false) purpose

Adrian's former life as an advertising executive means he's implicated amongst the guilty of selling a false sense of purpose. He was once sent out on to the streets of Manchester in early December with a microphone to ask people in a crowded town centre, 'What do you *really* want for Christmas?' The supermarket brand who'd commissioned him were hoping people would say, 'I'd *really* like a large TV from the Acme Supermarket.' Maybe it was how Adrian asked the question, or a particularly reflective bunch of people, because many of them had their heads in a different place entirely: 'I'd like to look after the homeless.' 'I want the fighting in the Middle East to stop.' 'Can't we help lonely people have a good Christmas?' were some of the answers. It was a moment when purpose for a supermarket and purpose for a person got mixed up. It's no wonder. Because we believe everybody is built to have a purpose that's more important than shopping.

Your mission statement

You may never have thought of coming up with your personal mission statement, but many companies do — they're everywhere, trying to capture an organisation's reason for existing. And they can be a little lofty. Take this one from Starbucks: 'To inspire and nurture the human spirit — one person, one cup, and one neighbourhood at a time.' Or this, 'To embrace the human spirit and let it fly' — that's Virgin Atlantic.

You'd think this next one was a political party — 'To create a better everyday life for the many people' — but no . . . it's IKEA. Pretentious? Surely not. Try this from Coca Cola, 'To refresh the world in mind, body and spirit. To inspire moments of optimism and happiness through our brands and actions. . .' Hmmm.

What would your mission statement be?

> Be yourself, everyone else is already taken.
> – Oscar Wilde

Shopping for meaning

Something very powerful has happened inside the heads of our generation. Most of us have not had to fight any wars, we've benefitted from property booms, and we've swallowed the lie that meaning comes through acquiring stuff. We've heard many describe their hobby as shopping, and it is a recognised addiction.

Choose Life. Choose a job. Choose a career. Choose a family. Choose a fucking big television; choose washing machines, cars, compact disc players and electrical tin openers. Choose good health, low cholesterol, and dental insurance. Choose fixed-interest mortgage repayments. Choose a starter home. Choose your friends. Choose leisurewear and matching luggage. Choose a three-piece suite on hire purchase in a range of fucking fabrics. Choose DIY and wondering who the fuck you are on Sunday morning. Choose sitting on that couch watching mind-numbing, spirit-crushing game shows, stuffing fucking junk food into your mouth. Choose rotting away at the end of it all, pissing your last in a miserable home, nothing more than an embarrassment to the selfish, fucked up brats you spawned to replace yourselves. Choose your future. Choose life ... But why would I want to do a thing like that? I chose not to choose life. I chose somethin' else. And the reasons? There are no reasons. Who needs reasons when you've got heroin?

— Irvine Welsh, Trainspotting[6]

Purpose vs anaesthetic

Our drive for meaning and purpose is strong, but it can be seduced by consumerism and other things. When we lose touch with our purpose, we hurt ourselves. It's as if we've lost our satnav. Act 3 is a particularly vulnerable stage. The midlife crisis cliché isn't a cliché for nothing — it's common and can be a terrible experience. And when we hurt it's easy to reach for anaesthetics.

When the right thing is wrong

Any activity, however noble, can prevent us finding our purpose, including 'meaningful' occupations like religious professionals, doctors, nurses, therapists or coaches.

As the son of a clergyman, Adrian knows several religious professionals who have given away more of themselves than they could sustain, resulting in anger, depression, divorces, damage to their key relationships, bitterness, addictions and illness. It could be that the very meaningfulness of what these people do is in fact their anaesthetic. The same could be true of the medical, therapeutic, teaching and other vocational professions. No one is immune.

Your anaesthetic could be fitness, DIY, fishing, socialising, football, gardening, music, eating, drinking, drugs, travelling, gambling, sex, religion, shopping, reading, procrastination, self-improvement and a yachtful of other activities.

> My biggest problem is I just keep myself far too busy. What am I avoiding?
>
> – James

What's your poison?

Find somewhere comfy to sit where you do not usually go — maybe a different café or park bench — anywhere that will allow you to listen to yourself.

Ask yourself: 'What do I do to insulate myself from feelings of discomfort?' Judy's anaesthetic is a glass of wine or mindless scrolling on Twitter. Adrian's is comfort eating and drinking . . . Make a note or draw yours.

What would it be like if you could spend less time with the anaesthetic and more time with the part of you that longs for purpose? Note or draw how that would feel.

In Act 3, as you become more aware of your mortality and that time is limited, perhaps due to a crisis, you ask what has the real you got to give to the universe while there's still time, and how will you do it?

Arthur Pooley, 67, decided to join a group of people who walked from London to Jerusalem.

Some of the inspiring people I met had been doing inspiring things in their day jobs, they didn't have to wait for Act 3 to do that. I felt quite ordinary in what I do in Suffolk, and I felt quite ordinary in walking to Jerusalem.

It would be rather sweet if others thought it was inspiring, but for me it was just a succession of Sunday walks. It took 5 months; we had one day off a week.

Here are some questions to help you uncover your purpose further.

How do you locate purpose?

To start to locate your purpose you first need to find a place where you can be on your own to reflect, it could be walking, sitting, anywhere you can have a conversation with yourself.

Write or draw your purpose in your Act 3 story

Read these questions through, and pick at least three that appeal to you:

- Ask yourself, as a young person my ambition as an adult was. . .
- In Act 3, with time to be still and dream, I imagine myself. . .
- The last five occasions when I was truly happy were . . . (List or draw them 1, 2, 3, 4, 5)
- I lose track of time, engaged in an activity, when I am . . .
- Set phone timer to ping in 90 seconds. Write everything you love doing before the bell . . .
- How would your 3 best friends describe you? . . . (If you don't know, ask them)
- Imagine you're in a group of people watching someone on stage. The person talking is really going down well with the audience. Because of what the speaker is saying the room is excited and energised. You suddenly realise that the person holding the crowd captive . . . is you. What are you speaking about? . . .
- Star in your own film: write one paragraph describing you as the hero of your own movie picking up from where you are now and ending in an extraordinary place.

We hope this uncovers a better story of yourself than the one you are used to telling. It takes courage to imagine and then act on being a better you. It's safer and easier to stay in your comfort zone, but less fulfilling.

I am two-time Golden Globe winner, Jim Carrey. You know, when I go to sleep at night, I'm not just a guy going to sleep. I'm two-time Golden Globe winner, Jim Carrey, going to get some well-needed shut-eye. And

> *when I dream, I don't just dream any old dream. No, sir.*
> *I dream about being three-time Golden Globe winning*
> *actor, Jim Carrey. Because then I would be enough. It*
> *would finally be true. And I could stop this terrible*
> *search, for what I know ultimately won't fulfil me.*
>
> *- Jim Carrey*[7]

Jim Carrey's tears-of-a-clown speech is surprisingly candid. His admission seems to say that he is programmed to strive after more and more awards, but deep down he knows this isn't going to be ultimately fulfilling. It doesn't give him purpose. Others are pointing this out too — Brené Brown, who has one of the top five most viewed TED Talks in the world (currently 42 million views), says 'A lot of stories we tell ourselves just aren't true.'[8]

If the stories we are telling ourselves about who we are and what we're here for just aren't true, it's time to tell ourselves new, true stories. Especially in Act 3.

Purpose sustains. Mortality prompts

At any stage of your life, but particularly in Act 3 as you become more conscious of your mortality, the more you connect with purpose, the better you'll thrive.

Another way to find and build purpose

Here's a tool to think about it which comes from the Japanese concept of *Ikigai*, where purpose is described as a balance of:

- what you love
- what the world needs
- what you're good at
- what you can be rewarded for

'IKIGAI'*

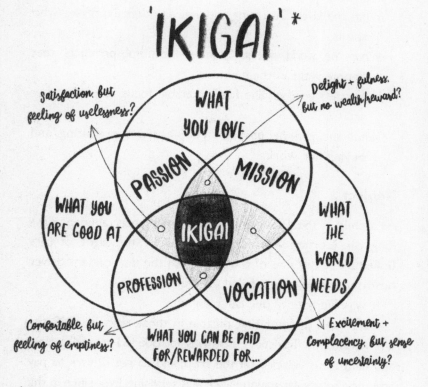

satisfaction. but feeling of uselessness?

Delight + fulness. but no wealth/reward?

WHAT YOU LOVE

PASSION

MISSION

WHAT YOU ARE GOOD AT

IKIGAI

WHAT THE WORLD NEEDS

PROFESSION

VOCATION

Comfortable. but feeling of emptiness?

WHAT YOU CAN BE PAID FOR/REWARDED FOR...

Excitement + Complacency. but sense of uncertainty?

*IKIGAI: JAPANESE CONCEPT — 'A REASON FOR BEING'

You might find it helpful to do your own version of the *Ikigai* diagram to help discover your purpose. Beware thinking that 'What you can be paid for' only amounts to a financial return. In Act 3, it's much better to think of this as 'What gives me reward?' – because what you do needs to be sustainable.

We spoke to a former professor of children's dentistry, Ruth Holt, who in retirement took several art degrees and is now a textile designer and weaver. Her story could be applied to the *Ikigai* model:

What she loves: Designing and weaving that expresses who she is.

What the world needs: Creative beautiful products that people want in their homes.

What she's good at: She has incredible focus to perfect her art.

What she can be paid for: People are appreciating and buying her work.

Neglect

As a child in the 1950s and 1960s, family entertainment on a long car journey would be provided by the sight of cars boiled up at the side of the road with the despondent driver head-scratching over a failed engine.

It was funny, until our car blew up.

Cars were just not that reliable in those days. In 1960 the UK Ministry of Transport Test was introduced to get useless and dangerous vehicles off the road, and to get drivers to pay attention to regular maintenance and servicing. Ever since in the UK, any car over 3 years old has to be MOT tested annually.

Your sense of purpose might change over time, which is fine, but when we neglect what we're really here for we're in trouble.

This neglect might have happened because of busyness in Act 2 or because 'I don't feel I have the right' or you feel it's just navel gazing. Don't worry, this is normal.

You might need to junk what you've got and start over with a new sense of purpose, or remind yourself of a purpose that you've lost sight of.

Look what happened when Maggie rediscovered her sense of purpose through music in her life. As she says, it became, 'one of the most significant things I almost didn't do'.

When I was about 10, I wanted to swim the English Channel or marry a farmer and have ten children. Neither of these fantasies worked out, thankfully.

After a degree in Music and English I found myself in a dream job as a video producer, script writer and music composer. I was very busy working in a creatively fulfilling and more-than-full-time job.

In my late 40s, it was time for some kind of change, and I felt the need to communicate more directly and meaningfully with audiences. So I booked on a jazz summer school, not expecting anything special to happen. But it remains one of the most significant things I almost didn't do. My life in music opened up in ways I had never envisaged. Two singers and I formed a vocal trio and gave concerts throughout the UK. I'd always wanted to be in a band, so that was a dream come true and provided great companionship. I composed for several community musicals and started a term-time workshop for anyone who wanted to sing, was invited to conduct and arrange pieces for local choirs.

It hasn't been plain sailing since then, but I know that music is really important for my health and for the health of the people I work with.

I am 65 as I write this. I want to keep on working on creative projects for as long as possible. I love the contact I have with younger people and think this is a *really important way of staying fresh and in touch with life and vitality.*

What's important to me is to find the answer to the question, 'What is your heart's desire?' and to follow that and try to act on it.

I would like to be remembered as someone who cared, and whose music, in some small way, brought health and well-being to people. As Beethoven reportedly said, 'I leave my music to heal the world.'

- Mags Stuart

How to understand yourself better

It's a bit of a rude shock when you own up that you don't really understand yourself, let alone your life partner, for instance. There's a range of tools that help with understanding yourself. The one that we have found very useful in our relationship for nearly 30 years is called the *Enneagram*, and it's helped us make sense of ourselves and each other.

Enneagram

The Enneagram is an ancient tool to understand the nine interconnected personality types and how they relate to each other. We cannot go into this here as it would take us off on another whole journey of discovery, but if you'd like to investigate it, take a free test online and/or buy some books. Suggestions are listed in the back of this book.

One-minute summary: Purpose

What are you here for? We are creatures with heart and it's a mystery.

Something stirs deep within when we love deeply, accompany someone as they die or stand in awe at some extraordinary natural event – a sunset, the first warm day of the year, maybe the birth of a grandchild. Or music, art or an overwhelming experience hits you and makes you weep. When you are deeply touched, what do you think your heart is telling you you're here for? People who have discovered their purpose seem to make their own electricity.

Finding your purpose in life before it's too late is probably the most valuable use of your time and energy in Act 3. If you knew this was your last day on earth, what legacy do you want to leave? Get on with it . . .

We had the experience but missed the meaning.
– T. S. Eliot, 'The Dry Salvages'[9]

Root 3 – Values

If we are to go forward, we must go back and rediscover those precious values.
– Martin Luther King, Jr.[10]

Why do values matter? We've made values a root because without them your tree is in danger of falling over, especially in Act 3 when your days may be numbered. Living a life that is not true to your values is a recipe for warped growth and disappointment. We have seen this happen. It's a big reason why we wanted to write this book. We've met too many people who've never considered their personal values.

What are values?

Values can be thought of as your moral compass. They describe *how* you do what you do and they drive your behaviour. 'She went about the redundancy process in a very *careful* and *respectful* way.' Or 'The way he made the redundancies was *thoughtless* and *hurtful*.'

We agree the V word is tricky. Values are often mentioned these days in the corporate world – but loosely – and ironically, the word 'values' has itself been devalued.

Workplaces are littered with lip-service 'Values Statements' where the words can bear little relation to actions or feelings.

A world-famous brand's stated values are 'Integrity, Leadership ... Passion for Winning, Trust', yet a senior ex-employee confessed:

There is enormous pressure to go with the crowd, so if someone tries to stand up to internal corruption, distortion and dishonesty, the greater likelihood is that they will be blackballed and punished, not rewarded.

– Anonymous

Sometimes people know exactly what their values are, but lack of awareness, self-esteem or courage prevents them acting on their values.

I found certain friends at the gym good company and fun to be with. I went along with it for a while, but their bitchy and spiteful side began to dominate, and it made me feel uncomfortable. So, I took a liberating decision to stop seeing these toxic people. I decided they weren't actually 'friends'. What I really wanted was more honest, kind friendships where I could be myself.
- Sarah

It's sometimes easier to identify what our values are when they get denied, as Sarah found. For example, if honesty and integrity are important values to you and then someone lies to you, a button is pressed, it will upset you.

A principle isn't a principle until it costs you something.
– Bill Bernbach[11]

Where do values come from?

Values are often borrowed or inherited from parents, the group, culture or religion you grew up with – they are ways of behaving you absorb and you find hard to give up. They create a voice – like a parent – shouting (or whispering) in your head.

> *'You should always do your best.'*
> *'You should never trust a stranger.'*

Watch out for that word *'should'*.

When Judy works with parents, she always asks them what values they want to pass on to their children. A parent once said, 'Surely every parent says the same thing, they want their kids to work hard, be kind and respectful?' 'No, they don't,' said Judy. 'What parents want for their children differs greatly. Some parents see academic success as important at any cost.'

In families, we see fridge magnets and cushions proclaiming 'Love is at the Heart of Our Home' or 'Kindness is King', but what we see and hear in families can be anything but.

Values can change

We grow our own values too, and over time they can change. In the early years of our married life in the 1980s, we paid no attention to recycling or bottle banks. Glass bottles would get chucked in the bin along with everything else. Thirty years on, we have a mini-recycling centre in our kitchen and huffy words are exchanged if anything goes in the wrong bins, let alone putting the wrong bin out on collection day.

A growing value of ours now is the importance of care for the planet. Watch out for that word *'important'*.

Going commando

Commando Chaplain Stu used to accompany his troops into battle. On one occasion in Afghanistan his commandos were fighting the Taliban in a fierce firefight, and Stu was alongside. Anticipating this earlier, he had taken a decision to take the pressure off the guys in the platoon – before they left base, he showed them the pistol he was taking into battle to look after himself, so they wouldn't risk their lives in battle and worry about him.

It was only after they were safely back from enemy lines that Stu revealed that he had put no bullets in his gun. 'I hate guns,' he said.

The man who went into battle with no bullets in his gun, prepared to pay the ultimate price, honoured his values: caring, responsibility, respect, self-sacrifice, courage, non-violence.

He had identified his values.

How will you identify yours?

We know people by their actions

'She felt a bit low and lacking energy but the school expected her to help with reading every week, so she still turned up.'

'Every time we met he asked me about my kids, remembering all their names.'

Consider what values are in action in these two examples.

Using your journal, describe someone as if to a mutual friend only by listing their *actions*. Then consider what it tells you about their values.

What values are important to you in Act 3?

Have a look at the following values list to help you see what personal values matter to you most.

Adventure

Assertiveness

Caring

Cleanliness

Compassion

Confidence

Consideration

Courage

Courtesy

Creativity

Decency

Determination

Empathy

Enthusiasm

Excellence

Fairness

Faithfulness

Flexibility

Forgiveness

Friendliness

Fun

Generosity

Gentleness

Health

Helpfulness

Honesty

Honour

Humility

Idealism

Innovation

Joyfulness

Justice

Kindness

Love

Loyalty

Mercy

Moderation

Modesty

Obedience

Orderliness

Patience

Peace

Purposefulness

Reliability

Resilience

Respect

Responsibility

Reverence

Self-Discipline

Service

Simplicity

Steadfastness

Tactfulness

Thankfulness

Tolerance

Trust

Truthfulness

Unity

Of the values you've listed, which ones do you want to prioritise? Can you pick your top three – the ones you can't live

without? Maybe some of your values have been asleep for a while.

Could you parent these children?

Simon and Dorothy – at 55, their own three children having left home – decided to adopt a sibling group of three young children after seeing an advertisement that said 'Could you parent these children?' Now in their early 60s, we spoke to them about the gains, and the challenges of starting again as parents, and adopting in Act 3.

Dorothy: *We'd said to various people that we were looking forward to the empty nest, but seeing the advertisement, I was surprised; I experienced it as a real finger-of-God moment, 'Could you parent these particular children?'*

We'd had a little experience fostering a teenager who was known to our family. That was quite challenging but also quite rewarding, and I thought we probably could parent these children. I thought we'd be too old to qualify, but that turned out not to be a problem: it's really hard to find anyone who can take three children, and we had evidence as experienced parents that we would be able to cope. We are well resourced here; we knew that our house, our family, but also the community where we live is a very easy and pleasant place to bring up children.

We didn't look at any other children. The whole process, from reading the advert to the children moving in took six months.

Simon: There was a sense of calling; this was very unusual for us. I can't really explain why that came about or why I felt so convinced. Had they turned us down we probably wouldn't have sought other children. We would have gone back to going on cruises (laughter).

I think it's quite hard to say, even with your own children, what is so rewarding about being a parent, because it's easier to think about all the things that are difficult. They are delightful children. There's something quite rewarding about having a small child who, when they're distressed, comes to you, who wants your love and support.

Dorothy: It's nice to have something new to do together at this stage of our lives. I've found it interesting to learn about the issues of adoption and two of them are twins, so that's been another bit of interest. For me anyway it is a long game and we're still at the stage when we're still building a lot . . .

Simon: There is a sense of satisfaction – at my age everybody thinks, 'What am I doing with my life?' I've been at Microsoft for 20 years and that's a long time to be in one job. If you look back over the story arc of what you've done with your life and think, 'What am I doing with my life beyond just carrying on with it?' . . . this is really something. We have done something together that – however it turns out, and we don't know how it'll all turn out – the children's chances are bound to be better than they were. At a deep level that's quite rewarding.

It's given us a lot of purpose. When people ask, 'What do you do?', previously I probably would have majored on work. Now I start with the children because it's a big part of my life. At 60 I feel like I'm just getting going.

Dorothy: We don't need to go on cruises or play golf all the time. We went on some nice holidays in the few months before the new children came, and that felt like enough – we don't need to spend another forty years doing that.

A big challenge is that it's so tiring, but having said that in many ways I think I'm in better shape than I was in my early 30s – I have more stamina and look after myself better now. I found it quite difficult cycling along with them at first, they were like a box of frogs! When it comes to that sort of thing, your age shows. On the other hand, you're much more mature and therefore more relaxed in all sorts of ways – that makes it much easier as you know what you're doing.

When you get to your deathbed, do you think you'll have any regrets?

Simon: It's something we've decided to do. I don't think it's a decision we'll regret at all. They push us outside our comfort zone. There's a tendency as you get older to get more and more into your comfort zone and things gradually calm down.

In taking on these children, it's a way of saying we want to keep pushing at something that will not allow us to deteriorate with age.

Dorothy: There is a risk. We used to say with our other children, 'Well, they're fine now but this time next year they could all be on drugs.' Things can happen with your own biological children. Things can still go wrong. There's just a risk involved and with adopted children there's a higher risk.

You can have a fantasy about doing something really wonderful instead of doing head-lice combing, or laundry – there is a sacrifice – and sometimes I find that quite difficult. But that's always the case when you make a choice.

If anyone in Act 3 was thinking of doing the same thing, what would your message to them be?

Simon: My message would be it's great! It's a good thing to do. You should really think about it carefully because it does give a whole new set of life chances to a child. And that's a huge gift that you are able to offer. You just need to think about whether you have the resources to do it. I don't mean mainly money, I mean time and energy and a support network. Our parents have all died, which contributed to our being able to do this. Lots of our contemporaries are busy looking after their parents – that was something we weren't doing.

It is a big commitment. No doubt about it. Act 3 people have capacity, they've still got the energy, they have time, enough money. That's a rich thing to be able to offer.

Dorothy and Simon's story certainly shows them finding a great renewed purpose. As we said before, there is sometimes overlap between values and purpose. Their story demonstrates the values they want to live by as they move through their Act 3. Those values are kindness, generosity, courage, risk taking, selflessness, commitment, hard work and endurance.

One-minute summary: Values

Your life is ruled by values: yours or ones you've inherited. They dominate your thinking with words like:

'Should' 'Ought' 'Must' 'Right' 'Wrong'

Act 3 is the time to define *your* values. Without knowing what matters to you most, you're vulnerable to living by somebody else's ideals. Enough 'shoulding'. Give yourself permission (at last) to follow your heart and live by the rules that matter most to *you*. That will give you the best shot at creating an Act 3 life you'll be delighted with.

> Those are my principles and if you don't like them
> . . . well, I have others.
> – Groucho Marx[12]

Root 4 - Key Relationships

Umuntu ngumuntu ngabantu.
(A person is a person through other persons.)
– Zulu proverb[13]

The fourth root of your tree is key relationships.

Thinking about key relationships is not easy. Whatever we say, it feels like someone could get hurt or offended. Causing upset, judgement or pain is never our intention.

If reading this creates painful feelings, highlights loneliness, heartbreak, destructive relationships or a source of fear, we urge you to take care when you see this symbol.

Taking care of yourself

Taking care could mean facing the truth you are now discovering about yourself when you still have time to change it. It could also include seeking professional help. (See resources section at the end of this book.)

Thinking about key relationships can make you feel a sense of wonder and gratitude for the benefits that come from giving and receiving love, care and attention, to and from a partner, family member or special friend. But it can also be a reminder of just how difficult one or more of your key relationships is.

What is a key relationship?

On workshops we run, some people question what we mean here. We think it includes someone who accepts you as you are, and listens without judgement. Someone you can be vulnerable with; someone you can trust, who brings out the best in you, and who you could probably call in the night if needed. It doesn't have to be all these elements, nor does it need to be a family member. We have known people who feel they are unable to say their partner or spouse is a key relationship.

Why do key relationships matter more in Act 3?

In Act 3, key relationships take on deeper meaning and significance as you feel gratitude for shared miles. If you have had a special friend or family member in your life for more than 50 years, that's over 18,000 days you might have been with them or thought about them. It's a lot of birthday cards written. It could be many hours of tears and hugs by now. It could be the most intimate relationship: your life partner who knows every inch of your body, and how you like your tea. These valuable souls in our lives who are our peers also start to feel the signs of ageing as we do. We compare notes about aches and pains. We sit with one another through worrying health issues. We might look at our nearest and dearest at this point, and ask ourselves, 'Will you be at my funeral or will I be at yours?' We have wondered that.

If you have children, they are likely to leave home, perhaps find partners and start their own families, extending the network out to include grandchildren. That's been the goal since you first held them in your arms, but now, does that empty nest hurt or feel like a result? It's often both.

On the upside, you may relish the comfort of being with old friends, who've have travelled with you over many years. New key relationships are the possible bonus of developing different interests or a move to a new area. It's never too late.

So, we're talking about those you love. Deeply love. Unconditionally love. We're not talking about 528 'friends' on Facebook or 7,000 Twitter followers.

Perhaps you can't think of anyone you would call a key relationship and you are feeling lonely. We are very aware of how difficult it is and how much it can hurt to be lonely. Loneliness is also found in partnerships and friendships, and it's very tricky to have to face up to this. As in all feelings, the first step is to acknowledge them, and that is also the first step to finding answers. It can take time, and sometimes professional help to deal with this once loneliness has been acknowledeged, but it can be done.

> *After my husband left, I still had lots of good friends and family, and to a few, I was the second person they cared about most. But I was no longer anyone's number one.*
>
> *- Eliza*

Is there one person who matters a bit more than anyone else? Someone who strengthens your Act 3 tree?

Key relationships - the truth

 Some of this might make uncomfortable reading. We're putting the following truths in here to highlight just how serious the issue of loneliness is, before we move on to some solutions.

There's a deluge of studies about loneliness, especially at this time of our lives. The fact is, good relationships keep you happier and healthier. It's backed up by a 75-year study on adult happiness by Harvard Medical School. There's a great TED Talk by Professor Robert Waldinger on this.

The UK government has recently appointed a Minister for Loneliness, because doctors see between one and five patients a day who have come mainly because they are lonely.

In the UK, 200,000 people over the age of 75 regularly go a month without speaking to a relative or friend. Dame Esther Rantzen founded the Silver Line, a helpline offering advice and friendship to older people. Launched in 2013, it now receives over 10,000 calls a week with 53% saying they literally have no one else to talk to.

This growing problem of loneliness amongst older people is upsetting and not what helps the individual or communities. It is certainly not what this layer of our society deserves, to feel shoved out of the way.

So, with that in mind, it will help you and the health of your Act 3 tree, to do some work on the whole topic of key relationships. That might mean taking stock of the ones you have, keeping them warm and mutually beneficial, or it might mean moving towards initiating one. Which will require action.

If you can't think of anyone who you'd call a key relationship, we hope you'll carry on reading and that the ideas below will encourage you to move towards a place where you can change this.

Why should I make all the effort?

Sometimes you feel resentful if you are making most of the effort to look after key relationships or initiate them. Disappointment and sadness come from expecting that people will seek us out. In our experience, not all friendships are mutually satisfying. Sometimes it just  feels one way, and again, we can lose a lot of sleep over resenting this. It's important to acknowledge how you feel, and equally, to do what you can to *make a move towards people*: don't give up, especially in Act 3.

Take action to make friends

Here are some ideas that do help. You might know some or all of them, and we include more as this chapter goes on. If you feel you really don't have anyone you would call a key relationship, we hope something here will help you.

In our workshops, we ask people to call out answers to 'Who is the perfect Act 3 person?' Here are some of the qualities people mention.

We all know perfection doesn't exist, but sometimes it helps to have an inspirational list. You could do the same for the qualities you want to find in key relationships. The most important thing comes down to finding people with shared values, so that's a good place to start, by going back to values you wrote earlier.

Here are some other ideas:

- Think about your interests, and where you could find like-minded people.
- Sign up for a class.
- Activities – meeting people alongside each other, rather than face to face. For example walking groups, volunteering, sport or recreational pursuits.
- Neighbours – more on this in the home section (in Chapter Five). Meanwhile, how could you get to know them better? Can you invite them round, or be more proactive speaking to people in the street?
- Online – Lumen is a dating site specially for the over 50s.
- Faith groups – we see many people trying out religion in Act 3, or going back to their faith from childhood.
- Move – a big one, but a house move could give all sorts of benefits, including meeting new people. More in the home section, including co-housing.
- Share your home – could you have someone move in?
- Write about being on your own. Blogging or social media could help you process your feelings and find other people who resonate with you.

What else? Ask around, try ideas out, something is probably better than nothing as Amelia Thomas discovered. She was widowed when her husband died in a car accident.

Just a year after my husband died, a great help was a ten-week evening class I took. This was so exciting and sent me in a new direction. I now organise classes in this area.

Who are your key relationships?

In the turbulence of family life, sometimes it feels like the only beating heart that loves us unconditionally is the family pet. Dog owners know that no one else runs down the hallway to greet them when they come home.

We loved our family dog and he felt almost as special as a person, and it was devastating when he died.

But when it comes to who helps you most in your life, it's human friendship you need – especially in Act 3.

Who's in your circle?

We want to give you the opportunity to evaluate your key relationships, but this is very much a 'take care' moment, when you need to find the right time and place and answer these questions in your journal.

- Who accepts you as you are, and listens without judgement? Someone you can be vulnerable with?
- Who do you trust the most?
- Who brings out the best in you?
- Who would you call in the night if you needed help?

They might be family – your partner, children, parents, siblings or other relatives. They might be one or two significant friends, neighbours or colleagues. Who is it?

Your circle

Copy the circles diagram into your journal.

Put your initials in the centre circle, then consider who is closest to you and put in their initials to join you in that circle.

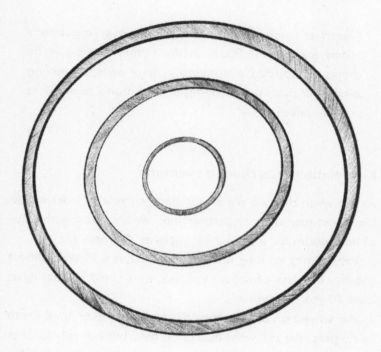

Who would be in the next circle out?

And the one beyond that?

If you can't think of anyone, then who would you like to develop a better relationship with?

What would you do to boost your social life? (Have a look at the ideas above.)

What would be the first step?

> Completing the circles exercise made me see I had more close relationships than I realised.
>
> — Simon

> Doing my circles exercise, I realised that my husband is not in my inner circle. It made me cry.
>
> — Hannah

I spotted I needed to invite people over regularly. I opted for the last Friday in the month - open home drinks. It stopped me giving energy away to feeling pissed off that I wasn't being invited round as easily as couples seem to be.

- Paula

Key relationships change over time

As we write this, we are in our thirtieth year of married life. Like most marriages or partnerships, we set out together full of enthusiasm for a shared life together. A whole *life*.

We're living so long now, you wonder, is a lifetime almost too much to ask of today's couples, who could be sharing at least 70 years together?

We vowed on our wedding day to be together 'until death us do part'. We still want that to be true, but our relationship, in common with many other couples, is a potent mix of joy and struggle. We are very different people. It takes work. We don't mind saying we have sought help from a relationship therapist to maintain and improve areas of our marriage. Like us, you might know of people who have changed over time and the relationship doesn't always survive the change.

Some couples can appear to have a much more charmed relationship than might in fact be true. It is, as the Chinese proverb says, far more common to experience issues.

No one can hang a sign out saying
'Nothing the matter here.'
– Chinese proverb

No one knows what really goes on behind closed doors, and of course you can be lonely in a relationship. Our observation of long, contented relationships shows us that focusing on helpful communication, patience, understanding, forgiveness, kindness, humour and respect go a long way.

Maintain your relationship

Our boiler and our car have an annual service to prevent them from breaking down. Here's what one couple do to keep their 44-year-old marriage on the road.

> *Every year we put a day aside for marriage maintenance! It is an essential time for us to talk through our hopes, challenges and plans for the year. We both think ahead, so we come with ideas and an agenda. It's too precious to just busk it on the day, and we make sure we go away somewhere else, not just sit at home.*
>
> *We talk about work, money, family, our home and our souls – our deepest part. Sometimes we have to say something hard, but we commit to keep talking until we can find an answer. This work on our relationship fuels the year. It keeps the glue that sticks us together sticky. We keep notes too and it's been fascinating for us to see over the years how decisions have worked out, like deciding to downsize and leave London.*
>
> *- Derek and Dawn*

Relationships take trust on both sides, work and commitment if they are to survive, or even thrive, on the long road of Act 3, and maybe Act 4.

Journalist Angela Neustatter and her husband found their 40-plus-year marriage was in trouble once the kids left. They nearly split up, but instead, made a self-contained area each in the family home. Their marriage was rebooted and saved.

As we said, the definition of key relationships is yours to decide. Yet the principles of looking after those relationships apply across the board.

What if you have kids . . .

Being parents in Act 3

We are parents to three grown-up daughters, who have now flown the nest. We started planning for it some years back, working out when our youngest could be ready to go, and how old we would be by then – practical stuff, really. But when the last child left, it brought an avalanche of mixed feelings. Relief, sadness, pride and some uncertainty. A new hush in the house that was deafening at times. Meals for two, eaten quietly, more notable silences. Food lingered in the fridge. It took days to create enough laundry for a load.

Kids leaving home, for whatever reason, turns the page in your family story.

We've had our kids in the house for 27 years, so us both adapting to this new stage isn't going to happen overnight. Single parents tell us it's yet another moment when their singleness dominates.

But it's not all gloom and doom.

Upsides of empty nest

There are many – here are the headlines we have found.

Freedom – fewer needs and wants to consider, which opens up gaps in the heart, mind and diary.

Spontaneity – walk out the door, say yes to more last-minute options.

Reinvent – your career, your interests or time for you.

Reconnect – with friends and family near and far, and your partner.

More money – possibly, or the chance to reduce the cost of living.

An opportunity to offer resources to others – rent out a child's bedroom? It doesn't have to be full time. Monday–Friday, for example.

Downsizing – is now the time to think about moving?

Less clutter – lack of overflowing laundry basket and stuff to trip over.

We have owned and faced up to our empty nest feelings. We are trying to be kind to ourselves and each other – it's OK to cry, to feel a bit rudderless. Our kids know we miss them, but that we're OK too. And they're welcome home any time. They will always have a key.

However, you may still be caring for children, for all manner of reasons, from having children later in life, new relationships, adoptions or raising grandchildren.

Women continue to have babies well into their 40s. Men into their 80s. The number of women over 50 in the UK having children has doubled in the last five years.

Writer and film maker Naomi Gryn had her first child at age 51:[14]

The downside is, predictably, tiredness and money worries. I need to stay fit. I've even stopped cycling, because if I had an accident, it would be catastrophic for all three of us.

I miss having my own space and being able to concentrate on work. My freedom has been curtailed and sometimes I miss the spontaneity of single, childless life, but not as much as I thought I would. It's been a blast, and I love it all, even the really irritating or stressful bits.

Boomerang kids

Boomerang kids are adult children who come back home because it's too expensive to leave, or their own relationships don't work out, or they can't find work. Or because they get fed, clean pants and a listening ear.

Unlike previous generations who couldn't wait to leave home, many of us have good relationships with our adult children, and find ways to adapt to cohabiting with each other.

Manage expectations

Where we see it working best is when house rules are agreed early and regularly reviewed, especially when it comes to money and helping out.

It's about understanding and negotiating all the *needs* and *wants* of everyone living under the same roof.

The key skills for relationships apply here too – see below.

> *At 28, it's hard to live with the people who used to brush your teeth*
>
> *- Sarah Marsh, living at home again*

Parents and siblings

All our parents have died. Judy's dad just dropped dead one day at the age of 73. Her mum was diagnosed with Alzheimer's the same year, and it took 9 years of the most painful decline before she finally died.

Losing a parent is huge – even if your relationship was rough. Even if death is expected. Or wished for.

When parents die, the loss of the layer above you is deeply felt – you're next in line. There can be sadness and regrets for what was never said. We have a friend John who'd had a troubled relationship with his dad. He says:

> It had been difficult - until Dad's second wife died the year before, she had always come between us. But once she'd gone, we had a good period of time together to slowly say goodbye - to thank each other. He had a good death.
>
> - John Bright

In our work, we have seen all the damage parents can inflict too. But the regret factor here is very high when parents die leaving open wounds behind.

This next exercise needs some careful time and thinking space, as will the one about siblings.

It's a chance for you to think about what, if you could, you'd want to say to your parents before it's too late. Can they die, and you live on in peace, knowing you had a chance to clear the slate between you? This is very

TAKE

CARE

sensitive. What if what you wanted to say is devastating to them? Maybe you won't actually say it, but it's important to acknowledge it at least to yourself, and also what, (if anything), has been good.

Forgiveness is important – as the saying goes, 'Not forgiving is like drinking rat poison and waiting for the rat to die.' Forgiveness can bring huge relief.

According to the Mayo Clinic, the health benefits of forgiveness are improved relationships, decreased anxiety and stress, lower blood pressure, lowered risk of depression and stronger immune and heart health.[15] Letting go of negative emotions can often have a remarkable impact on the body.

Here's an exercise that can help you take care of unfinished business between you and your parents.

About your parents

Write, without taking your pen off the page, all the things you'd like to say to your parents before they go. Try not to think too much about this – just write from your gut. If they have died, still do it.

'Why can't you be more like your brother or sister?'

Judy has heard this unhelpful comparison from parents far too many times in her coaching work. The sibling relationships are likely to be the longest ones in your life. That can be a scary thought if you have had many years of not getting on – living with jealousy, competition and comparisons. Sadly, we have come across many people who are estranged from their siblings, and who say things like *'We never did get on, and I don't care if we never see each other again.'* Only you will know your true feelings from your experiences, but what we see is that reconcilliation between siblings can often be of great benefit.

On the upside, your relationship with your siblings can be the best one you have – maybe no one else understands you like they do, no one else finds the same family jokes funny.

Even though the relationship patterns between brothers and sisters might have been running for decades, if they are destructive, we find in Act 3 it is more important than ever to try a reboot, before it's too late and one or more of you is left with regrets.

I had the most extraordinary and very honest conversation with my brother about Act 3 type matters last night. It was really big stuff and all in the context of Mum not being around any more. I think that because of what we did in the Act 3 weekend workshop, I was able to have a different level of conversation. He is retired and did a lot for Mum since he stopped working. So he now has big choices such as where to live, as his house will not be suitable longer term. Plus the whole 'what is life? / time running out issue'. We are beginning to build a new relationship where there hasn't been much of one during our 'Act 2s' as we have led very different lives to date. That conversation made me realise we do have more in common and that it is important for me to actively nourish this relationship. Green shoots of hope are showing, so that's a good thing.

- Gill , 51

We were particularly struck by Gill's sentence *'that it is important for me to actively nourish this relationship'* as it shows her willingness to be proactive, and not wait for him.

About siblings

As you did for parents, write without taking your pen off the page all the things you'd like to say to your siblings before they die, or you do. Try not to think too much about this – just write from your gut. If they have died, still do it.

TAKE
CARE

Both the parents and the siblings writing exercises can stir up big feelings. The value of doing them is that, at the very least, you are owning up to your feelings on the page, even if they are difficult and painful, or perhaps you're not proud of what you wrote. You may have been holding this stuff in for a long time, but what we know is that it is more important during Act 3 to address these things while you still can. It's even more important to take care of yourself, and seek support from people close to you or professional help.

More ideas on how to look after your key relationships

We've sat in the room with people suffering stress, agony, disruption and health crises that come from key relationships being in trouble.

The ideas below may look like a statement of the blindingly obvious, but years of coaching, studying and our own experience shows us these things are still essential for healthy relationships. Any of us can forget or overlook sound principles. Maybe we just don't want to face up to what's needed.

Problem ownership

This is a tool which many find helpful to determine who has the problem in the first place. The clue is who got upset first? If it's the other person, the most useful thing we can do is to listen (see below for listening skills). If we're upset, we can ask for help, using an 'I' statement, such as *'I am upset that you booked tickets without asking me first as I have to visit Mum that day.'* If both sides are upset, it's a shared problem. That will need both of you to calm down, and to agree how best to resolve it, focusing on solutions, not blame or shame. Using the problem ownership tool can be a brilliant way of sorting out disputes with anyone, including children.

Say sorry

Say sorry without justification. Just sorry, because someone is upset, even if you think they don't need to be. *'I'm sorry you're upset.'* It's hard if you think you're still right, but what you are apologising for is not necessarily what you've said, if you believe it to be true, but the *effect* that it's had on the other person. It's much more useful to wait until you are both calm to sort out a difference of opinion.

Flexibility

In Act 3, our bodies can struggle with stiffness, as can our minds; we can get more entrenched in our views. However, having a flexible and open mind is more constructive, and sometimes the way to foster this is by using your pause button – see below.

Intimacy

It's a word that people see differently. What is your idea of intimacy? What is just for the two of you and no one else? There is a mutual interdependence on each other, mentally, emotionally and physically. It can include sex, which can be tricky in Act 3, but it can also be the best time for sex, in part because the worry of a potential pregnancy has gone. Intimacy is an area that needs care, with respectful conversation, and that may need professional help.

Kindness

Ask yourself, especially when resentment is brewing, *What would be the* kind *thing to do or say now?'* Or say nothing and just listen.

Trust

You are in this for the long haul. Trust isn't built overnight and it deepens over time. Both sides need to decide that the other is worthy of trust. You might have a problem with trust in one area, spending money for example, but that may not mean someone is therefore untrustworthy with the children or with being faithful. Over many years in a relationship, trust can ebb and flow, but it's important to keep talking about it, and believe in the relationship through both the dark and the light days.

Honesty

Being free to be yourself, without hurting the other. Honesty can clear tension, but it must be handled with care and with respect for the other person. (See the problem ownership idea above.)

Try something new

The experience of learning a new skill, or visiting a new place together can inject fresh energy.

Humour

Sometimes the shared jokes will be the best bit . . . but if it's all been too serious for a while, you could try to remember and rekindle what you found funny in the early stages of your relationship. But humour is subjective, so be careful when it moves to making fun of someone and turns sour.

Listening is the best thing you can do in a relationship.

In our workshops, we get people to practise the listening skills below.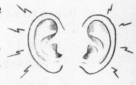

They often say how powerful it is to experience being truly heard. That means their feelings have been taken seriously, and therefore they feel understood and accepted.

How to be a good listener

- Take the speaker seriously. Imagine they know more than you. This establishes respect between you.

Body language

- Aim to be relaxed, calm, rested, fed and watered. Sit on chairs at the same level, opposite and facing each other with arms unfolded. However, sometimes it's more productive to listen side by side, such as when walking or on a car journey.
- Eye contact shows you're paying attention — but it might be that the other person doesn't want to meet your gaze or you sense it feels too intense. Don't worry about that, it is already helpful to simply have your caring presence.
- Paying attention to their body language and tone of voice. What is the person telling you through their body? For example, are they hunched? Fidgety? Is their breathing fast? Are they sweaty? All these are clues to someone being anxious, ill at ease or burdened. Is their voice quiet, loud, panicky, quavering? How is it different to their normal voice? *'You have a lot of tension in your shoulders, I'm wondering what's bothering you?'*

What to say

- Try to imagine the emotion they are feeling, and vocalise it. *'Your son not returning your calls sounds really frustrating.'*
- Ask open questions which means they can't be answered with a 'yes' or 'no'. Instead, begin questions with a who, what, how or when.
- Wait for a pause, and don't interrupt their flow. When you do speak, keep away from advice, fixing their problem or 'Me too', which means jumping in with your story. This is about them and their story. Your job is to just listen.

The sound of silence

Silence doesn't mean there is nothing being said. On our workshops, we sometimes just put up a picture of our dog — he was often the best listener in the family.

Get better at listening

- Look at the good listening points above, which one do you want to prioritise in your key relationships?
- What stops you listening? Write it down

When you're doing this kind of listening, beware of your own strong feelings and reactions that might prevent further listening. For example, something that presses a values button.

> *My husband and I were discussing what kind of wedding our daughter wanted to have. When I realised he was more interested in the public show of the wedding than the small wedding she really wanted, I couldn't bear to listen to him any more. It was all about him - not her.*
>
> *- Deborah*

What stops you listening?

- **Values clash:** *'I can't believe you think that matters.'* Hearing people that matter express different values to yours, or the ones you thought they held, presses a button in you and makes it very hard to listen.
- **Disrespect:** this could be either the listener or the speaker, and can shut down either side or create anger and resentment.
- **Heard it all before:** the familiarity of old arguments can easily breed contempt, as can the way they are expressed, the language used and the tone of voice. *'I've been saying for years that boy will never amount to anything!'*
- **Wrong time, wrong place:** being too busy, too tired or in the wrong location will shut off listening.
- **Jealousy / resentment (no one listens to me):** if you feel unlistened to, it can really get in the way of your being able to listen to somebody else.
- **Judgement:** you might believe or even know they're wrong, but listening isn't about who is right or wrong, it's about understanding each other's position or feeling, before you can move on to what to do about it.

- **Trying to fix or suggest:** as above, jumping in with advice, suggestions, changing the subject or fixing their problem can stop you hearing what they are trying to say to you.

I Want to Hold Your Hand

When sex gets too tricky,
When our words sound too bland,
Let's do something simple;
Put your hand in my hand.

When truths lie unspoken,
Yet we both understand,
Move close on the sofa;
Put your hand in my hand.

When darkness surrounds us
And the nightmares expand,
Roll over to my side;
Put your hand in my hand.

When I start to shuffle,
When when my strength sifts like sand,
Walk closely beside me;
Put your hand in my hand.

When my breathing gets shallow,
When I make my last stand,
Pull up to my bedside;
Put your hand in my hand.

— Steve Turner[16]

Relationship tool – The Pause Button

Sometimes when tension is mounting and tempers are rising, it's easy to say something you'll regret. A tool our clients have found helpful is to use their pause button. That is they do something conscious to calm down, and then respond more usefully.

Ways to use your pause button

Have a look at these ideas and see which ones you feel could work for you.

Come up with a simple phrase; for example:

'I need to think about that' or

'I'm feeling quite upset, I need some time to calm down and let's talk after supper.'

In an argument, try saying: *'We need to both calm down before we can talk about this any further.'* You may then need to leave the room or if you're somewhere confined, insist you put the conversation on hold until you're both calm.

Physical ideas:

- Take 10 deep breaths
- Go outside – walk round the block
- Get some exercise: dance, sing or do some star jumps
- Do something creative
- Chop or punch something harmlessly
- Sit down

How would you press pause?

Write the words you'll try, or use your own ideas to press pause.

Key relationships – what would help you?

Go back over the tips, think about your key relationships. Which tips, if you really focused on them, would help?

One-minute summary: Key Relationships

 Love each other. It's as simple and as difficult as that. Here's how:

Love is patient and kind,
Love does not envy or boast,
It is not arrogant or rude.
It does not insist on its own way,
It is not irritable or resentful,
It does not rejoice at wrongdoing,
but rejoices with the truth.
Love bears all things, believes all things,
hopes all things, endures all things.
Love never ends.
– The Bible, 1 Corinthians 13:4–8[17]
(Read at more weddings than anything else)

Chapter Four

Health and the Science of Growing Older

Health is not valued till sickness comes.
– Thomas Fuller[1]

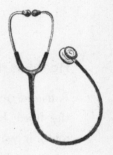

In every workshop we've run about Act 3, people have raised two overriding concerns: health and money. We've met people who don't want to be rich, but no one (yet) who says, 'I don't want to be healthy.' That's why we've made health the main trunk supporting our Act 3 tree. Without it we're dead. Yet millions in later life are ignoring their health. Or walking into the future backwards.

In this chapter we focus on how we can take simple steps to become healthier and fitter through exercise, diet, relationships and sleep. This will usually mean a change of thinking and behaviour.

Ask the Doc

As we are not health experts, we asked Richard Vincent, an Emeritus Professor at Brighton and Sussex Medical School, to write this chapter. Richard is a highly experienced speaker and travels all over the world helping doctors to be more effective at patient care and communication. He's got some useful understandable health points for us in Act 3, and although you might know lots of this stuff, sometimes it helps to be reminded.

Richard says about himself: *I spend much of my time helping doctors to be really effective – and to stay well themselves. Here's a very short summary of things that might be useful for you to know about health and fitness in Act 3.*

What is health and how do we get there?

Health is a state of complete physical, mental and social well-being and not merely the absence of disease or infirmity.

– World Health Organization[2]

Health is much bigger than the body's machine

A friend once hit a squash ball hard into my eye. I reeled to the floor, hitting my knee. My injuries hurt, but so did my mind. It was dealing with both my pain and my fears about what would happen next. Would my eye be damaged? Would our friendship suffer? Our conversation, though still friendly, wasn't quite the same as it had been a minute earlier.

Any injury or illness will in some way strike at us **physically**, **mentally** and **socially**. Usually, in more serious examples, sufferers find **spiritual** concerns rising up as well. All four of these dimensions are key to maintaining or restoring our health, not only the body's biological nuts and bolts.

Ageing and illness - breaking the link

Ageing is more complicated than just 'wearing out'. Over time, the endlessly active trillions of cells in our body gradually change the way they work. They lose water, which makes our limbs stiffer and more brittle and reduces our height and weight. Our DNA loses its capacity to replace our cells when necessary, particularly when they decrease more rapidly after middle age.

Our immune and defence systems change, too. As we grow older, they become weaker against invaders but more likely to treat important parts of us as though they were foreign. Healthy cells get chewed up as a result.

All these changes make arthritis, heart disease, cancer and diabetes much more common in later life. That's the bad news.

The good news

The good news is that many of these effects can be delayed by a healthy diet, effective exercise, strong relationships and good sleep.

Fitness and exercise

Those who think they have not time for bodily exercise will sooner or later have to find time for illness.
– Edward Smith-Stanley[3]

By not even taking a 10-minute brisk walk once a month, 6 million middle-aged people in England threaten their health.

> 41% of the 15.3 million English adults aged 40 to
> 60 walk less than 10 minutes continuously each
> month at a brisk pace of at least 3 mph.
>
> – Public Health England[4]

How fit are you for your age?

Here's a test that shows how strong you are in your lower body – your quadriceps (the front of your thighs) and your gluteal muscles (your bum) are the biggest muscles in your body:

Use a hard-seated chair and get a friend to hold its back and to time you. Sit with your arms crossed over your chest, placing your hands on the opposite shoulders. How long does it take you to stand up and sit down again ten times as quickly as you can?

- Men under 35 should take 10 seconds or less.
- Women under 35 should take 12 seconds or less.
- Men under 55 should take 13 seconds or less.
- Women under 55 should take 15 seconds or less.
- Men over 55 should take 18 seconds or less.
- Women over 55 should take 19 seconds or less.

Lower your risk

Beyond maintaining our fitness for everyday activities, exercise reduces the likelihood of heart disease, stroke, cancer, dementia, depression, diabetes and immune deficiency diseases. If you do it well, you can lower your risk of all these by about 20%.

Exercise works for good in two ways

Cardio and Movement – aerobic exercise: Exercise based on movement gradually increases your pulse rate, blood pressure, breathing and circulation. This improves the efficiency of your heart and lungs. Joints are kept active, balance mechanisms are kept in trim and muscles are invigorated. It also promotes natural sleep.

Lifting and pushing – anaerobic exercise: Heaving up weights, or generating pressure in some other way, provides short bursts of exercise with little movement. Breathlessness begins quickly, triggered in a different way from aerobic activity. Exercise of this kind primarily increases muscle strength and stability – worth having to maintain capability even for small tasks such as opening jars or lifting things. It also keeps bones healthy and prevents falling over.

How to exercise: Making yourself out of breath at least once a day is probably enough to maintain day-to-day fitness. Exercises that involve whole-body movement – 'cardio' – are much better for this: for example, fast walking, swimming, running, cycling or playing sport that gets you out of breath.

Wanting to be fit and well for ordinary activities, while prolonging our life as much as we can, is not the same as being super fit with big muscles. If the latter is your aim, you'll have to put in much more oomph, including substantial anaerobic workouts.

Walking is good: Write down in your journal how far you walk every week for a month. Note week 1, week 2, week 3 and week 4.

If you don't know how to measure your steps, download the free app *Active 10*, and tally your steps. If you're very inactive, aim for at least 10 minutes of brisk walking every day. Think: 'I could easily do that if, instead of using the car, I walked my regular routes (or at least part of them).'

Even better, go for ten minutes of very fast walking 3 times a day on 3 days a week. This would give you your optimum benefit.

Or do something shorter and more exciting each day: say 10 minutes of high intensity exercise (HIT):

- 2 minutes of running on the spot
- 2 minutes of squats
- 1 minute of star jumps
- 5 minutes in total
- Repeat

Dancing is great: As well as boosting our metabolism, dancing tickles up the brain and stimulates the memory. Balance, strength, coordination, attitude, purpose and relationships are all improved. And it's fun!

Using muscles for good balance: One of the greatest sources of injury as we get older is falling over. Judy fell on the stairs today, due to absentmindedly running up to get something she'd forgotten. Easily done, but the bruising will take a while to calm down, and she is determined to try to remember to always hold on to the bannisters.

The 30-Second Balance Test: This will assess how well balanced you are (physically . . .)

Find a partner to time you and to check your safety (your eyes will be closed, and you might fall). Then:
1. Stand barefoot on a hard floor, eyes closed.
2. If you're right-handed – lift your left foot 6 inches off the floor. If left-handed – use your right foot.

3. Your partner times how long you can hold that position without wobbling or opening your eyes.

4. Repeat the test 3 times. Add up your total time and divide it by 3 to find your average balance base. (For example, if test 1 was 4 seconds, test 2 was 8 seconds and test 3 was 6 seconds, you'd add up 4, 8 and 6 to get 18. Divide that by 3, and your average balance time is 6 seconds.)

What's your actual balance-based age?

Improving your balance: A simple and quick method to improve your balance that needs no longer than two minutes, is to stand on one leg while cleaning your teeth. This training will lessen the likelihood of your falling over whatever you're doing. (It doesn't necessarily work with dentures.) Adrian's

WHAT'S YOUR ACTUAL BALANCE—BASED AGE?	
BALANCE TIME	**ACTUAL BALANCED—BASED AGE**
4 seconds	70 years
5 seconds	65 years
7 seconds	60 years
8 seconds	55 years
9 seconds	50 years
12 seconds	45 years
16 seconds	40 years
22 seconds	30–35 years
28 seconds	25–30 years

balance-based age was older than his actual age, so he now stands on one leg every time he's in the bathroom.

You don't need a gym subscription or special equipment: Simple but effective exercises can maintain a good level of fitness without recourse to a gym. Yet for some, exercising with others, and in a positive environment, brings real benefit.

What will keep you going?

The key question is about your incentive and motivation. Will you keep at it? Attending exercise classes or being active with friends can help, and some people use heart monitors and apps to record how much their body is benefitting from exercise. Positive feedback keeps us going. (A point of interest: UK gym members waste £600 million in annual fees because of abandoned attendance.)

The exercises suggested in this book can be free, or low cost, and require very little 'apparatus'. A chair, a wall, good footwear, light rain-wear and possibly a bike and a swimming costume provide the main exercise kit for most.

Have a long-term goal: Perhaps you are trying to lose weight or get fitter? Going up stairs two at a time would work, but it might take several months to reach your objective.

Or have a goal for the day: Having a goal for each day is much more achievable. This might be to complete the exercises already mentioned, or a number of other short-term changes in your routine. With wearable technology (Fitbit, for example), you can set yourself an activity-related number and aim to reach it every day.

Wearable technology isn't perfect: Recent studies have shown that many people get very attached to their wearable technology and wouldn't be without it. However, it has the potential for a darker side too, as some users reported that any activities that were not recorded were wasted, or that they felt controlled by their gadget. Something to watch out for, perhaps.

Taking control

One retired desk worker, Jim Owen, looked in the mirror on his 70th birthday and didn't like what he saw:

> I'm overweight, my knees hurt and my shoulder is frozen. In 15 years, I'll be a disaster.
> — James P. Owen, *Just Move!*[5]

So Jim took control of his own body: In his eighth decade, he started an easy fitness programme that he does in his own home every morning – mainly exercises and stretching – with a few visits to the gym. When he started he could barely manage one push-up. Now, age 77, Jim is fitter than he was in school. His book, *Just Move! A New Approach to Fitness After 50*, is a useful guide to getting functionally fit in older age. Even better, his approach isn't about trying to look like mutton dressed as Arnold Schwarzenegger.

Spoiler Alerts!: Remember, simply having a target number of steps per day isn't quite as effective in keeping track of your activity and fitness as the exercises described above.

Long-term self-monitoring with digital devices can result in negative as well as positive effects on fitness behaviour. Research has shown that some users feel under an existing external pressure to complete their targets and that their daily routines are being completely controlled by technology. Demotivation, feelings of guilt and even depression have been noted when a device persisitently reminds them of their failures. Others feel that any exercise that is accidentally unmonitored is wasted.

Eating

Moving from Act 2 to Act 3 is a change of life – a major transition. You'll make the most of your opportunities for the next 30 years by adjusting your habits of exercise and eating. Permanently.

You're slowing down: Your metabolism has been slowing down since you were 20. In Act 3, it's time to eat your age: 2,000 calories for a woman and 2,500 for a man. Your body needs less food – so lower your intake.

Overweight: Being very overweight (that is, technically 'obese' with a body mass index of over 29.5) is frighteningly common; and it shortens life. In the UK, 26% of adults and 25% of 10/11-year-old children are classified as obese. In 2016–17 obesity was a contributory factor in over 600,000 admissions to NHS hospitals. Don't go there, and don't go for a short-term diet. Strike out for a permanent change of menu.

Healthy eating: Follow the plant-rich Mediterranean diet, shown from studies in over 1.5 million people to lengthen your life and reduce your risk of cardiovascular disease, cancer, Parkinson's disease and Alzheimer's disease. Women who eat a Mediterranean diet supplemented with extra virgin olive oil and mixed nuts may also have a reduced risk of breast cancer.

And remember:

You can't out-exercise a bad diet

What to eat: A healthy diet is very straightforward:

- Reduce saturated fats (in dairy and meat products).
- Olive oil is king!
- Whatever you do, try to reduce sugar. Sugar is more dangerous than fat. Part of the reason is that, when stored, sugar gets turned into fat – including the wicked cholesterol.
- Eat less red meat: once a week or less is good. Poultry, egg white, fish and milk give you the same or more protein but affect body fat and weight more favourably.
- Put fish high on the menu. Fish has good fatty acids for brains and the heart – especially oily fish, including salmon, mackerel, sardines or trout.
- Adrian has had success in losing weight through Slimming World. It works.

Fibre is vital to keep things moving: There are two types of fibre: insoluble, which won't dissolve in water (high in cereals and the majority of vegetables); and soluble (mainly in oats and fruit). Eat both. The fibre found in fruit is particularly good because of its beneficial effect on heart disease, stroke and diabetes. Vegetables are also good, improving the mechanics and possibly the biome (the healthy bacterial culture) of the gut.

Alcohol: The long-held view that a couple of glasses of red wine will do you good is now dismissed. Here's a quote from the *British Medical Journal* in October 2018, reporting extensive global research: 'The level of alcohol consumption that minimised harm across health outcomes was zero.'

The good news is that this is not the same as saying you shouldn't drink, but it does emphasise the potential risks to body, mind and society of having 'just one more . . .' Taken in excess, the well-known adverse effects of alcohol are both immediate and long-term. The brain and liver suffer most, with personal health and often social consequences.

Forget Food Supplements: Unless medically advised, forget food supplements – in spite of their massive marketing. Vitamin D has been greatly hyped, but we have enough in an ordinary diet. Unless you're stuck in a mine with no sunshine or experience long, dark winters, the amounts we need are tiny. You might need it in the treatment of osteoporosis. But in general, if you're eating normally and going out at least sometime every day in daylight, you're fine. Recent research suggests that even the current NHS recommendations for the routine vitamin D supplementation for children and certain adults may be outdated.

Vitamin C is fascinating. Its level in our blood is very tightly regulated. Too much can be problematic, so that the body rejects high doses even before they are absorbed. Does it ward off colds or inflammation? No. Not according to clinical trials. But it might make you feel better, because of a placebo effect. (Placebo effects are real and can be very powerful – respect them!)

Massive amounts of vitamins and other supplements are marketed, particularly for older age groups. Self-prescribed, these are likely to benefit their suppliers more than their buyers.

How to eat

Don't eat too much of anything: Ideally, have a very good breakfast (omitting the cooked bacon and sausage – sorry), a smaller lunch, and little in the evening. This pattern certainly lowers cholesterol absorption and fat accumulation. If you have a big meal in the evening, you're likely to store its calories and fat rather than burn them up. Less food late in the evening may also improve sleep.

Eat slowly: This is much better for routing the nutrients you eat to their best place for storage in the body. It also enables the stomach to signal when we are full-up. We have a sneaky system connected to our brain which says, 'Time to stop!' But if we eat quickly, this doesn't have long enough to work – so we eat too much.

Other eating tips

It's helpful to drink a glass of water before your meal, to look at your food and to talk to someone while you eat.

Forgive yourself and carry on: It's hard to change lifelong eating habits, especially if you are a comfort eater. If you mess up, don't worry; forgive yourself and carry on with what you know is healthy. Keep coming back to it. It will take time to establish new habits, but you will.

Mind – the gap

The gap in our understanding between our bodies and the workings of our minds is huge, but it's clear that they are intimately connected. Fortunately, advanced scans and chemical studies of the brain, along with observations of

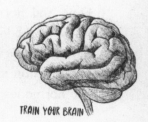

TRAIN YOUR BRAIN

our behaviour and our health, are closing this gap with increasing speed.

Our minds process our thinking and feelings, and from these come our conscious choices of what we do. For example, we may decide either to go for a run or slump by the fire, either to eat a cream cake or munch a raw apple. And, as we have been exploring in this chapter so far, many such behavioural choices can influence our health through pathways we now understand.

But our minds also influence our bodies in ways that are less obvious. They exert powerful effects using chemical and electrical signals to influence the background processes that keep us well and protected. A familiar example is what happens if we are caught by a sudden fright. When our mind interprets a sight or sound as an imminent danger, it activates a package of emergency measures triggered though the brain. A range of hormones is poured out: adrenaline, noradrenaline, oestrogen, testosterone, cortisol, dopamine, serotonin – and several more. Our 'slow-down' hormones, however, are switched off. Together, these changes have a strong effect on every system in the body, including the control of blood sugar (raised) and immunity (lowered). This reaction is great for an emergency, but if sustained, it would prove increasingly detrimental.

It's not just in a crisis that the mind initiates these signalling systems; milder but longer-term emotional states, particularly challenges (conscious or unconscious), can result in brain and hormone activity that produces adverse effects. These might include alterations in immunity, blood flow and blood pressure, gastric function and our risk for internal inflammation in several different locations. Internal cannabis-like hormones may have a part to play here.

The traffic of signals between the mind and the body moves both ways, and their close interconnection plays powerfully into many matters of health and healing. Several examples are shown later when we consider loneliness, generosity, forgiveness and hopelessness.

Brain power: Our brains have about 100 billion cells, each creating up to 10,000 interconnections. Many of these form our distributed memory. Others manage all the body processes that either carry out our conscious commands – speak, move, smile, etc. – or control the background machinery that keeps us alive and well. It's a startlingly complicated system of digital electrics.

Left brain – right brain: Brains are divided in two halves, left and right, which are well connected across the centre. The left side deals mostly with language and logic, the right with emotion, intuition and creativity. Though we think that we operate life logically (with the left side in charge), it is often the right side that finally determines the choices we make. Both sides, using the strong link between them, play a key role in health.

The left side of your brain: The left side lights up if we experience an unusual symptom: pain, dizziness, tingling, whatever. Our logic tries to make sense of what's going on, and, accordingly, plans what to do – from nothing to calling an emergency ambulance.

We have discovered that what patients *think* about their condition has important outcomes. Their analytic thoughts about its cause, effects, likely duration and the chance of recurrence determine how they feel and what they do next, including whether they should seek help. Their thinking will also persuade them to take any prescribed treatment, or not, and it impacts strongly on how well they recover.

The right side of your brain: The right side, together with its influence on the left, supports our existence as persons beyond the mechanics of life. The creativity and imagination born there promote beneficial changes that develop mental, social and physical health. Children will spend hours and hours creating – a major contribution to their development.

Artistic communication, through music, art, writing or drama, nourishes us and extends our understanding beyond the confines of logic. In teaching doctors around the world, we often ask them to draw what it feels like to work in a particular setting or with a specific patient. Their informal art often reveals things they might not have found easy to express before, perhaps even to themselves.

Mental health - the big issue

> Depression is the single largest contributor to global disability that we have – a massive challenge for humankind.
>
> – John Geddes,
> Professor of Epidemiological Psychiatry,
> Oxford University[6]

The charity Mind has found that almost half the patients who consult their general practitioner do so for problems with their mental health, particularly anxiety and depression.

So, what can we do to avoid this? Much of the health advice we've discussed so far will have an impact not only on our physical health but also our state of mind – not surprising since our four 'dimensions' are tightly intertwined. Right-brain activities engage directly with our mental life, so making space for them is really worthwhile. Positive relationships also lead to more robust mental health. We will look at those shortly, but first let's consider a common experience and a commonly blamed cause of worsening mental health: stress.

Stress

The Stress Curve: A degree of stress is essential to get things done. It creates drive and energy. The more stress you have, the better you do – to start with. But pushing (or being pushed) more and more brings diminishing gain. You peak, then things begin to go wrong. After that, the curve goes down disastrously: fatigue, error, panic, anger, loss of self-respect, passivity and exhaustion can lead, in the end, to complete collapse.

What to do about stress: The first challenge is trying to sense when you're about to reach the top of the curve:

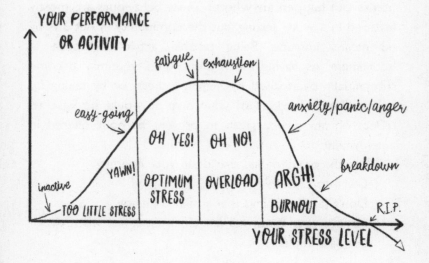

- How irritable are you getting?
- How well are you sleeping?
- How much do you feel like getting up in the morning to get on with things?
- Negative answers to these questions can be pointers to overload and burnout.

Spotting stress: Good friends may help by spotting and pointing out changes in your behaviour that might signal a coming landslide from excessive stress. These include:

- Arriving late and leaving early in attending anything that, even in a small way, could be demanding
- Recurrent sickness preventing a normal timetable
- Unusual rudeness
- Complaints from those with whom you interact
- Uncompleted and deferred tasks, causing an increasing number of errors
- Unusually erratic behaviour − flipping between highs and lows without reason

Stress can happen anywhere: These behaviours are mostly featured in a work setting, but the community in Act 3 is by no means immune. Being capable, active and seen in 'retirement' as having much more time, you may become substantially overloaded by helping others, or by taking up overambitious projects of your own. It would be wise to reflect on any advice given to prevent burnout offered in employment:

- Watch commitments that drain your energy
- Learn to say 'No'
- Don't take on things that you don't enjoy
- Manage your time well (i.e. clock time, not when the goal is complete)

- Have clear activity and rest boundaries
- Take control
- Delegate if necessary
- Take holidays
- And don't forget to exercise.

Health in the community

Relationships have a most powerful influence on our well-being. Go into a room and you begin to feel elated or wary, uncomfortable or at ease, according to who is there. The subtle chemistry that pervades the atmosphere impinges on your mental and physical health. Community is really, really important – as shown by many data.

Inequality: International research shows that in populations where the financial gap between rich and poor is wide, the health of everyone at all ages is less secure and life is shortened. More equal societies are healthier, but these are hard to create.

Relationships: Fractured relationships, through conflict or loss, cause psychological, and probably physical, pain. Think: if your resentment or fear subsided, you would be relieved of a burden, and your back pain, dizziness, whatever, would likely reduce.

The painful truth is that data shows the adverse effect of loneliness to be as powerful as smoking or alcoholism in threatening an early demise. If this is what you're feeling, don't panic, something can be done. Have a look at the ideas on loneliness in the Key Relationships section.

In contrast, a welcoming and supportive society that lives comfortably with a multi-age, multi-ethnic mix brings healthier lives in individuals of all ages: less childhood illness; better childhood progression; and reductions in coronary heart disease, cancer, infections, depression, dementia and premature death.

Showing empathy and compassion make us more healthy.

The art of giving: Understanding and generosity towards others reduces our own health risk, even if it doesn't always come easily. Substantial research demonstrates that giving enhances our quality of life and health. It reduces blood pressure as much as medicine or exercise and swings our immune chemistry into a beneficial pattern. It also lowers the risk of dementia, reduces anxiety and depression and improves the management of chronic pain. In a study of married couples, researchers found that the recipient of generosity expressed high levels of marital satisfaction – and so did the giver. Generosity also seems able to extend life: a study of 2,000 people in California found that volunteering dramatically reduced mortality rates.

The generosity of a smile, giving thanks or making genuine compliments works wonders for both parties – for free!

Go for forgiveness

One of the most healing phenomena is forgiveness: Sustained anger, resentment and bitterness are unhealthy, but forgiveness and working to overcome anger improves well-being mesurably. A study in 2019 reviewed data collected from a total of 58,531 subjects, and showed a significant and independent positive relationship between being forgiving and physical health. In a separate study of 32 patients with known coronary heart disease, forgiveness training was shown on cardiac scans to improve the blood flow to their heart muscle.

I have often seen people holding on to an insult which they refuse to forgive because their antagonist won't apologise.

The other person does the same. Such a deadlock causes a marked deterioration in mental health in both, often with debilitating physical manifestations as well.

Spiritual matters: We all have our own view of the word 'spiritual', positive or negative. We may take it to refer solely to the human spirit that defines and energises people as individuals or communities. Or more broadly, whatever gives us individual meaning and purpose.

Globally, around 6.4 billion people (84% of the world population) are estimated to follow a religious tradition. In almost every religion, following its conventional wisdom is advocated as the route to healing and health for both individuals and society. Extensive scientific observations over the past 20 years strongly support this connection.

In clinical practice, whether or not they adhere to any form of religion, many patients think that spiritual issues, however conceived, are important. Professionals treating cancer and heart failure see this commonly. But research has also shown that in 70–85% of patients with less threatening illnesses, spiritual issues are still held to be important.

Hopelessness: Hopelessness is more than a psychological symptom, perhaps bordering on existential. It certainly has a powerful effect on health. When it comes to the causes of a heart attack or cancer, a study of 2,482 men aged 42 to 60, who were followed for 6 years, showed that hopelessness turned out to be a bigger contributory factor than any of the classic culprits, including smoking.

Sleep

Night work: Sleeping away a third of your life could seem a waste of precious time for enjoyment or productivity; but without sleep we would die within twelve months. Research over 20 years has shown that our night-time period of 'rest' is filled with unconscious activity. Our bodies and minds depend on the machinery of sleep for a healthy and sane life the next day – and well beyond.

Sleep rearms: Physically, sleep rearms our immune function, promotes healing, balances insulin and glucose, regulates our appetite and weight, grows a beneficial microbiome pool in our gut and protects us from our big three threats to health: cardiovascular disease, cancer and dementia.

Sleep upgrades: The rhythm of sleep also delivers a regular and essential upgrade to our nervous system. Not only does it allow the transmission of our day's transient memories from the front of our brain to a permanent store further back, but it sorts, indexes and evaluates them to choose how best they should be filed.

Sleep soothes: In the last phase of sleep, 2 hours before waking, the memories of any event the previous day that caused emotional highs or lows are faxed to the back of the brain for special treatment. The factual data of these events are stored as usual, but the feelings they triggered are tempered and soothed. This enables us to recall past memories safely without experiencing the same intensity of emotion that erupted at the time.

Sleep is healthy: Sleep gives our psychological health a seriously good boost. Without it, anxiety and depression are more likely, and both our logic and creativity take a dive. If our waking day included skilled muscle actions and coordination, the ministry of sleep will ensure that the control patterns we used are shaped, polished and stored directly in the area of our brain that directs movement. The brain is the real site of the 'muscle memory' that hones our skills.

When sleep is missed: Against these life-enhancing benefits lies our costly habit of chronic sleep neglect. Regularly skimping on a full night's shut-eye hurts us both mentally and physically. Sleep deprivation also profoundly reduces our ability to learn. Staying up all night to finish something is counter-productive. Other people may suffer too — socially, financially or physically. At worst, think of the many thousands of traffic accidents and fatalities each year caused by drowsy driving.

But life will inevitably bring occasional nights of broken or missing sleep with little harm attached. The human frame is remarkably resilient. Catching up on a night's lost sleep seems best achieved by taking a 20-minute nap around lunchtime. Keeping to our usual times of going to bed and getting up preserves the important daily ('circadian') rhythm to which our body has become accustomed. And that's good!

Sleep lack — epidemic: The World Health Organization now declares sleep loss and its adverse effects as an epidemic raging across all industrialised nations. Its outcome is worse than the combined dangers of all recreational drugs and alcohol. But the recommended regular sleep period of 6 to 8 hours each night is threatened by many factors: the whirlwind of daytime activities (imposed or self-inflicted), artificial light everywhere, addiction to screens, the effect of stimulating chemicals, a distracting environment and too much heat. During the menopause or premenopause, nights can fre-quently be interrupted by episodes of wakefulness and intense body heat that reduce the quality and efficiency of sleep. A few people, usually men, will have a quite different pattern: periods of deep sleep associated with snoring, and sometimes pauses or gasps in breathing from partial obstruction of the airway. This problem requires medical attention. A doctor should also be consulted if insomnia is associated with either anxiety or depression.

The recipe for a good night's rest: If sleep is so important to body, mind and spirit, how can we achieve it? Here are some recommended steps:

- Count it essential to keep regular times for going to bed and getting up.
- If necessary, use an alarm clock for both ends of the night's rest.
- A relaxing ritual in preparing for sleep gets the brain cued up to switch into night-time mode. This is not the time to cram in a quick look at the emails or other 'essential' viewings.

Things to avoid:

- Caffeine – no tea, coffee, cocoa, chocolate or cola drinks for at least 4 hours before bedtime (6 hours is better).
- Nicotine – no cigarettes, vaping, patches or chewing gum for 1 hour before bedtime or when waking at night.
- Alcohol – taken around bedtime this can promote sleep at first, but it can also disrupt your slumbers later on.
- Eating a large meal immediately before bedtime (although a light snack may be beneficial).
- Eating in your bedroom.
- Making your bedroom too hot or too cold.

Things to do to aid sleep:

- Take regular (even mild) physical exercise daily, but stop at least 2 hours before bedtime.
- Try to spend some time in daylight (or bright artificial light) during the day.
- Keep the bedroom calm and tidy. Make it quiet and dark during the night. Select a mattress, sheets and pillows that are comfortable.
- Keep your bedroom for sleeping. Resist using it for watching television or other light-emitting screens. (E-ink readers work on reflected light, so should be less of a problem.)
- Listening to the radio or a podcast may or may not be helpful. For some, calm voices prove soporific; for others, gentle music works better.
- Check with your doctor or pharmacist whether any medications you have been prescribed might interfere with sleep or dreaming.

Lying in bed awake: If this happens close to getting-up time, snatch the moment and start the day. If in the middle of the night you can't get back to sleep after trying for 20 minutes, don't worry: get up and do something relaxing. (Screens with exciting happenings are off limits.)

If getting to sleep or staying asleep is becoming a persistent or worrying problem, do something about it. A chat to a GP would be wise. They may also be able to recommend a useful sleep app.

One-minute summary: Health

Take back control of your health. As you've seen, there is much you can do by changing your habits in Act 3 that will improve your enjoyment of life and reduce risk of disease. Surrender control and our health and vitality goes as well. People with control are healthier, have fewer sick days, weigh less and have less instances of disease. They live longer.

> Eat half. Walk double. Laugh triple.
> And love without measure.
> > – Tibetan proverb

Chapter Five

The Branches of the Tree

When you look at a tree, you see the trunk and the crown in all its glory. Outside the window in Suffolk where we're writing this today, there is a vast chestnut tree in full bloom, it must be ancient. There is no sign of the roots, but the branches and the trunk are wonderful.

Obviously, the roots are the most important part of *your* tree; they are what sustains you. The trunk of the tree, your health, supports a good Act 3.

But the *branches* are where your visible daily life is played out: the areas of friends, work, world issues, money, play and home. We're leaving an empty branch too, in case something else crops up for you.

People usually contact us about life coaching, when one of their branches is in trouble, such as a work issue, although they come to realise it's often the areas of the roots that need attention first.

In this section of the book, we'll go through what matters in each branch and how you can make your own Act 3 plans.

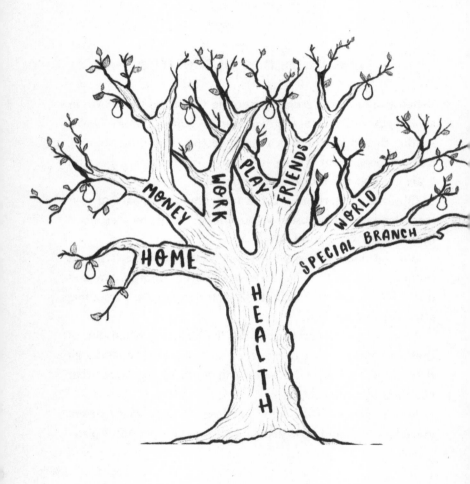

Branch 1 - Work

You owe it to all of us to get on with what you're good at.

– W. H. Auden[1]

Why do humans work? This is a funny question – after all, what is work? It's something that's so much part of the human habit that it almost seems daft to question it. But let's do it anyway, because our intention is to see what invisible ways work has been helping or hindering us in our Act 2 and see what's useful to bring out of that into our Act 3.

Work is a world of things
Is work just a way to pay the bills?
Is it just what you're paid for?
Is it a career?
Or a calling?
Or more?

Work is play: For some people – not just limited to artists and creative people – work is, in a sense, play. It is so absorbing and energising that it makes them more whole. They can't imagine *not* doing it. They can't believe they get paid for doing something they love.

Work is affirmation: Social reinforcement, adulation, praise, status, teamwork and affection – if received at work – are huge motivations to keep working. For example, how much status do you have at home compared to your professional world?

Work is power: You say it, they do it. Being in a position of power at work can feel great. This power is addictive. Power junkies love work, especially if when you're at home, even the dog ignores you.

Work is entertainment or engagement: The social side of the workplace for many is what keeps them there. A community where they are engaged and given a sense of identity. And believe it or not, some workplaces are incredibly fun.

Work is forgetting: Some use work to forget their daily reality. To blot out the present, to forget themselves and all they leave behind. For example, trouble at home with partners, children, ageing parents – especially our key relationships – can make work seem like a lucky escape or a holiday from personal difficulties.

Work is discovery and growing: It's not surprising that work is where many people meet their life partner, and learn life skills, practical and useful things, such as prioritising or negotiation, they might never have learned elsewhere.

Work gives meaning: It gives a reason to get up every day, clear goals to achieve.

Work is self-realisation: Work is a wonderful way to stretch a personality and discover hidden potential.

Philip Bier, who founded UK shop-chain Tiger, says:

You don't know your own capabilities unless you challenge yourself. It is quite liberating when you start thinking about what it is that is stopping you doing things. What goes on in your own head is probably the biggest block. If you can unblock that then you can do what you like . . . within reason.

Work is contributing: Many people see work as a way of making the world a better place.

Work is limiting: Some go to work to be limited, controlled, domesticated or parented. It's a place of security where they don't have to think.

Work is slavery: Sadly, many experience abuse at work, but feel powerless to speak out or react.

Work is hell: Some careers and some jobs are just hell.

Work is food and shelter: Let's be honest – many, possibly most, work just to survive.

Caring is work: Looking after children, parents, grandparents, in-laws, stepchildren, friends. Looking after homes. Sometimes relentless and mind-numbing, sometimes deeply rewarding.

Personal circumstance affects what work is possible: For instance, we've heard people say, 'I don't have a family, so I can focus entirely on work for as long as I can.'

Imagining a life without work is (almost) unthinkable:

Work occupies 35% of your waking hours over a 50-year working life.[2]

There's a clarifying scene in Martin Scorsese's *Taxi Driver* where Travis (Robert De Niro) talks to the older taxi driver Wizard (Peter Boyle) to understand his own disillusionment. Wizard replies:

> 'A man takes a job. That job, y'know, becomes what he is. You do a thing, and that's who you are. I've been a cabby for 17 years, 10 years at night. I still don't own my own cab. Why not? Must be because I don't want to. It must be what I want, y'know – being on the night shift, driving somebody else's cab. Understand? You get a job. You become the job.'
>
> – Paul Schrader, writer[3]

You get a job. You become the job: You easily slot into the job and after a while your picture of yourself defines and controls you. *'It must be what I want.'* Well, what if it *isn't* what you want?

And it may not be literally a job that takes you over: it could be a role you've fallen into as a parent, a relationship, a position in the community.

Loss of work: When you stop or lose work that was giving you meaning, what next? It's imperative, particularly in Act 3, to return to your roots to rediscover what matters to you, your values and purpose. That's where you'll find the direction for new, fulfilling work.

Fear of changing our work: Studies have shown that the fear of losing a steady salary is quite often greater than the potential happiness of finding a different job you really love.

Breaking out of limiting work: Cambridge neuroscientist Professor John Hodges told us of his ideas to run a café in Act 3:

I thought about all sorts of alternative life paths which were non-academic. I thought ahead to when I'm 65 and I didn't want to be one of those rather sad older men and women in academe, who everyone does homage to at the meetings, but sort of wishes they weren't there. I thought that is not what I want to be doing. At the end of my Cambridge period, I felt very burnt out, devoid of ideas and yet the Ph.D. students kept coming and the pressure was to hold this grant and apply for that grant, and I had had enough.

At that stage, I thought of retiring, and doing something completely different.

I think I started to flirt with the café idea, even ten years ago in my 50s.

> Your work is going to fill a large part of your life, and the only way to be truly satisfied is to do what you believe to be great work. And the only way to do great work is to love what you do.
> – Steve Jobs, Apple[4]

You've got a whole new work opportunity in Act 3: A wonderful thing about the transition to this stage of life is you've got a chance to reinvent your work, if you wish. And by doing so, you get to reinvent yourself too. Exciting times.

Work can provide much, but not everything: There are limits to what work can give us, as James Hollis says in *Finding*

Meaning in the Second Half of Life: 'We cannot expect family and work to provide all nurturing and empowerment – it's too big an ask. We must do it for ourselves.' Remember your tree roots.

What about turning your world of work around?: One of the things we have enjoyed most about writing this book has been interviewing many people who are radically changing their working lives in Act 3. The professor of dentistry who became a weaver in her 50s; the video-maker who is now a dancer in his 60s; the lawyer who in her 50s retrained as a midwife. We explore their stories later on.

Who would you become?

Dentistry professor to weaver: RUTH HOLT **retired from teaching dentistry to return to art college and now has a studio where she weaves artworks.**

You have all these influences, all these pressures, and you somehow have got to get yourself out. It's not a matter of isolating yourself, but saying to yourself what do you really want to do. I have talked to so many other people and asked, 'What's really important to you?' and they can't or won't define it. Won't do it. Either they think it's an ego trip, or they think they can't, or just don't know, but I think it takes a good bit of fishing round. The other thing I felt when I was doing this, was how difficult it was to strip the 'oughteries' away (ought to do this, ought not to do that . . .).

Your dream working life

What work would make your day?: Just write freely for at least 10 minutes what the best kind of working life would look like in your Act 3 years. Dream. No 'should'-ing yourself. It might be something you're already good at, or something completely different.

Write:

- In your dream, what are you doing?
- Where? Who with? What can you see, feel, hear, touch and smell?
- What does all that do for your spirit?
- Read it out loud to yourself.

Next, reread what you wrote about your purpose and values.
- Write down your values that are related to work.
- Write down what is the purpose of the working part of your life.
- Lastly, combining your values and purpose, create a statement about work, perhaps your mission statement.

> *My Act 3 working life will see me being able to pay the bills until my pension kicks in. More importantly, I want work that uses my ability to bring out the best in others, particularly where eco issues are concerned. I want to keep energy and time to enjoy other parts of my life, and not give everything away to work.*
>
> *- Lucy, 57*

> **We spoke to Phil Johnstone, who gave up a successful career in PR to do earthquake relief work.**
>
> *I think sometimes, when we get to the last stages of our life, it's unlikely we'll say to ourselves; 'Good on you! You stayed in those tramlines. You didn't risk, you just hung in there!' In the last years of my life, I'll probably be saying, 'You could have risked more, you could have taken more chances along the way.' And I think most people will say, 'You know I could have explored more, tried more things, taken some crazy decisions, because generally things work out.*

Paid work or unpaid in Act 3?: A large number of Act 3-ers will need to keep earning, but if you don't, and the work you want to do is valuable to you and the world, does it matter to you that you're unpaid? Perhaps you don't need the money – some people in that situation give the extra away. (More to come on this in the Money branch of the tree.)

> What does the world need from me
> that only I can give?

What does the world need from me?: Some people really like this question. But does it have to be answered through work? In Act 3, some can down tools and not have to worry about an income, but for so many, it's more complicated than that. In coaching, we help people to think long and hard about how they could find paid work that's more meaningful to them, taking into account their responsibilities. If that is impossible for now, then finding meaning in the other areas of your life can alleviate a job that's less satisfying. For example, it might make more sense financially to keep the job, and make time outside of work to pursue meaning and purpose. It's about action.

Only you can decide this. Really driven artists, for example, would say that the world needs to see, hear or experience their creative work, that the world is a better place with their art in it. A confident artist will carry on regardless even if no one sees it or buys it . . . That's called purpose. But it doesn't just belong to those in the arts world.

Lucy told us:

I've been an accountant / Finance Director for over 25 years, but in my 50s, I have decided to take short-term contracts to free up time and space to pursue other things outside of work. I love watching tennis and going to see bands - time doing these things is more valuable to me than earning more money. Setting boundaries on the number of days I commit to paid work has had the unexpected benefit of allowing my long-buried, more creative skills to re-emerge and blossom.

Coming up are all sorts of examples of people adapting their working lives in Act 3 to be more satisfying to them, while they still can.

Remember the earlier quote . . .

If you always do what you've always done, you'll always get what you've always got.

Is this your *Sliding Doors* moment?: *Sliding Doors*, the 1998 film starring Gwyneth Paltrow and John Hannah, alternates between two parallel universes, based on the two paths the central character's life could take depending on whether or not she catches a train – creating different outcomes in her life.

When you think about it, how many small and big decisions have you made that affect your working life until now? All these things have brought you to this place. Whether you went to college or straight into work. A relationship that took you in a different direction or when you had family responsibilites.

Do you want to continue to let these experiences define you, or are you prepared to be more in control of your life while you've still got time and energy left?

What's the process of clarifying a new work direction?: You'll know by now that we'll refer you back to your roots: attitude, purpose, values and key relationships.

> Vocation does not come from a voice 'out there'
> calling me to be something I am not. It comes
> from a voice 'in here' calling me to be the person
> I was born to be.
> – Thomas Merton, writer and monk[5]

So – who were you born to be?: It's OK to make mistakes and take wrong turnings working this one out. Don't focus on how annoying it can be that some people have instant and long-term clarity about their calling. Hey ho.

Work snapshots

Juliette, the lawyer who became a midwife in her 50s: Juliette trained and practised as a lawyer, had a family, then went back to university, trained as a midwife and now works in an NHS hospital in North London delivering babies:

It's fantastic. I love being employed and working in a massive organisation, in a profession that has such a reflective element, in a way that I wouldn't have enjoyed so much, or at all, when I was younger. I suppose that the negative is the hours, night shifts and weekends, but I'm still in the honeymoon period so that's barely a negative. I'm very careful to prioritise my sleep, as I know that I could get down if I'm tired. I'm working in a very supportive environment with great colleagues, and that's the defining quality that makes it a positive and joyful job.

Dan the oil man who became a healthcare assistant: Dan worked as an oil geologist most of his life, but after he'd had a brain aneurysm, which was successfully treated by the NHS, he decided to give back and now volunteers one day a week as a healthcare assistant:

When I'm working on the neuro ward and people are having a hard time, I get my phone out and show them the pictures of my head when it was all messed up and how I looked when I was in their situation – I do this to encourage them. They'll get through it!

Just think how much I'd have missed out on if I hadn't done this . . .
– Isobel Webster, on taking a new career

Footballer to special needs teacher: Neville Southall, once voted among the top 10 goalkeepers in the world, has, aged 59, not settled for the quiet life but now works as a special needs teacher, and champions marginalised communities:

I've got a bit of flak because if I stick up for sex workers some people think I'm supporting the trafficking of women. That's stupid. It could be your mum, your daughter, your sister, your brother. You don't know who is doing sex work. I'm trying to get across what they actually do and the barriers they face.

Maths teacher to hat maker: Tricia Hamilton was a maths and physics teacher now she runs a hat-making business.

I was 30 years a maths and physics teacher. I enjoyed children and seeing their progress. In 2010 I made a hat, then out of that made a new career and business.

I've always been creative, but not had the opportunity to prove it until now. Divorce was the darkest place I'd ever been. But I discovered you can do creativity in a dark place. In fact that's probably the most creative time in my career. I could never have imagined this much explosion in creativity.

Rock musician to funeral celebrant: Ollie Gold wore skintight trousers on stage to persuade the world he was the rock god the 1980s needed. Now he performs to a different crowd, by conducting funerals in Cornwall:

I was a legend in my own lunchtime for a while; I got to headline a festival in a rock band playing to 15,000 people and have written with Gary Barlow, Chaz Jankel, and had my songs recorded by a bunch of folk.

Now, in my third act, I take funerals for a living . . . for the living. You meet people at their point of need and love them through the process and it is such a privilege.

Listen to your life . . . touch, taste, smell your way
to the holy and hidden heart of it.
– Frederick Beuchner, *Now and Then*[6]

Find your 'why':

> **It helps if you know *why* you're doing your work, says 60-something actor Andrew Harrison:**
>
> *I had an epiphanous moment recently when it finally dawned on my fetid brain that I didn't become an actor to become rich and famous but rather to act. Thus, broadly speaking, if I was acting, I was content. And it's no bad thing to be content.*
>
> *I'm irked by people who ask: 'What are you doing?' when you know the subtext of their question is: 'Are you famous? Are you successful? Have you done lots of film and television? Are you getting on? Do you have juicy anecdotes to tell me about being an actor?'*
>
> *We are not defined by success. Nor are we defined by what we do. It's something much subtler and more interesting than that – a little thing called 'Life'.*

Working just for money – without real emotional commitment – will rust your soul.

Who would you be if you moved outside your comfort zone?

So many people spend most of their lives living and working only within their comfort zone, choosing to stay where they are because they are terrified of the panic zone.

Yet, between comfort and panic there exists a huge, rewarding stretch zone. In Act 2, Isobel Webster was a trained counsellor, working unpaid from age 22 to 45. Then in her early 50s, after

her husband took early retirement, she found herself doing cleaning work and wondered, 'Is this all I have to offer the world before I go?' When she was given the chance through a friend to become the PA to a human rights campaigner, she was amazed. '*Do not* let this chance go ...' she thought, and grabbed it.

If the job description had included almost anything that I actually do, I would sadly have said I couldn't accept the job because I couldn't do any of that, computers and so on. Yet here I am doing it and loving it! I have been immeasurably enriched and I hope that spreads a little to the people around me in my life.

- Isobel, 58

Attitude pushed her forward. That's where the growth is.

How would work give you growth?

Following on from your exercise earlier to dream up your best working life – this is about how you could be changed if you achieved your dream while you still can. It starts by becoming aware of what you see as your comfort, stretch and panic zones.

 Draw three concentric circles: the outer is your comfort zone, the middle is your stretch zone and the inner is your panic zone.

List five work things you might do in Act 3 that might stretch you.

What would these five things do for your purpose and values?

Purpose is the essence of what I'm getting from my business in Act 3. Even at the weekend I have a reason to get up, because my blog goes out on a Sunday morning and I'm actually quite busy in a good way. The purpose that it gives me is that I am part of a team. We now have a team of 12, two of whom are my daughters, so I have daily contact with them, which gives me a huge amount of pleasure and purpose.

- Tricia Cusden, founded
Look Fabulous Forever, aged 65

Work is work: We have one more job for you. As with the other tree branches, you will see the progress you want by creating a great goal to get cracking on, taking into account what you have already written in your journal about work.

Your goals in work

Go back to your tree. Picture your goal as the fruit at the end of the work branch. Always check that what you want and write about in work serves your roots (attitude, purpose, values and key relationships) as you create your goals.

Setting G.O.A.T.S. goals for your work:
- Genuine
- Optimistic
- Achievable
- Timed
- Specific

Over the next 10 years, or before I die:
- What are my goals for work?
- Describe what that will be like, and what will it give me?
- What could stop me achieving this?
- What are the leaves (steps) needed to get there?

> Love and work . . . work and love . . . what else is there really?
>
> – Sigmund Freud[7]

One-minute summary: Work

For you in Act 3, work may no longer be important – you might be all done with it.

Or, a new world of work could rejuvenate you far beyond what you can now imagine.

Where will you start?

Branch 2 - Play

We don't stop playing because we grow old; we grow old because we stop playing.

– George Bernard Shaw[8]

Why is play important?

Bodies, brains, moods, attitudes and relationships are all built and improved by play at any age and at any stage – so in Act 3 it makes sense to review what play is doing for you.

What is play?

Dr Stuart Brown from the US National Institute for Play says it is the engagement in the act that matters, the escape from time. The outcome is less important.

What are the acts of play? We're not just talking about sport or games – and those are important – but also creative or leisure pursuits. We would say play includes being with friends, walking, visiting places you love, cinema, reading, writing, dance, music or theatre, and probably many other things. Some might call these hobbies, what you do in your spare time. It could be active, like going fishing, or that you're the observer, such as when you listen to music.

We asked people we know, and we searched for data to find out in more detail, what are the most popular pastimes for people in Act 3. There is little research at the moment, but what we noticed was some difference between what men and women prefer to do in their spare time. The graphic word clouds below represent some of the activities; the larger the type, the more popular the activity. This is not scientific, and there will be great variation across culture, region and resource. We're showing you this to help inspire you with what you could be doing.

One group of women over 50 came up with these play activities:

camping MUSIC DANCING reading Parks WALKING
YOGA hiking TRAVEL horseriding WRITING SUDOKU MARKETS
genealogy SEWING TV CRAFTS GARDENING babysitting
SINGING decorating KNITTING CINEMA PHOTOGRAPHY QUILTING
pottery SAILING friends VOLUNTEERING
GRANDCHILDREN CROCHET

A group of men in Act 3 came up with these:

podcasts WINES football sports CYCLING
COOKING galleries TRAVEL drinking BIRDWATCHING
MUSIC horseriding collecting poetry writing
writing scrabble fitness walking
entertaining granddaughter
READING DRAWING
language gardening
HISTORY

How do you play?

> Play is pointless and that's the point.

We know play is crucial for kids

Play is what builds children's brains for life, love and work. It builds neural pathways. It introduces them to a range of emotions, dexterity, social skills, problem solving and analytical skills — some would say it is more important than the schoolroom.

We forget play is crucial to make healthy adults

Well-adjusted adults played freely as kids — that's the finding of Dr Stuart Brown, author of *Play: How it Shapes the Brain, Opens the Imagination, and Invigorates the Soul*. He found a significant link between play deprivation in childhood and adult behaviour. Healthy play makes healthy adults.

Juvenescence

Something that helps keep adults playful is access to multi-generational experiences. In their book *The 100-Year Life*, Lynda Gratton and Andrew Scott write extensively about the benefit of this, called juvenescence.

In 2018, Channel 4 screened their second series 'Old People's Home for 4 Year Olds' in which young children spent time with residents in a care home, partaking in many activities 4 year olds would naturally do, such as playing games, dancing and sharing stories. Medical experts measured the ability of the care-home residents, men and women ranging in age from early 80s to 102, in mobility, memory and mood at the beginning and end of the series. In almost every case, the residents' scores had dramatically improved by having access to the playful lives of young children. The children also showed increases in confidence, concentration and consideration of others.

We have worked with adults who struggle to play, because they still carry loud internal voices of play being disapproved of by their parents who would say or imply *'Stop being silly'* or *'You're wasting time when you should be doing your homework'* or *'You're just showing off'*. This comes from a parental fear that play means their child won't reach their potential – we think the opposite is true.

It seems those who play the best, survive the best.

> The people in our 75-year study
> who were happiest in retirement had worked to
> replace workmates with new playmates.
> – Professor Robert Waldinger, Harvard happiness study[9]

In Act 3, we need to play more and play better to stay healthy and connected.

Play makes you smarter

There's a positive link between brain size, frontal cortex development and play. During play, the brain engages in 'simulations' and creates connections that did not previously exist. Compared to other animals, the human species spends more years in childhood, and therefore many more years in play – so perhaps that's part of the reason we grow smarter than other animals.

NASA hires players

Several US companies have found that the best problem solvers are not just those with the best qualifications from the best universities, but those who have used their hands in their youth — tinkerers. NASA finds this helps problem solving in adulthood — which is handy when your rocket is in trouble half a million miles up in space.

Play can help beat depression

Dr Brown conducted a year-long study that involved a weekly commitment by a group of women, referred by their doctors, who were depressed and unresponsive to antidepressants. Many were self-doubting, struggling with questions like 'Why didn't my marriage work out?' or 'Why don't I have more friends?' They were asked to do a 45-minute fast walk at 80% of their maximum heart-rate, 4 times a week. The first 3 months were difficult, but thereafter the positive effects of exercise, and doing it as a group, began to show — a lessening of their depression and improved overall well-being. To maintain the benefit, they needed to keep this exercise going. It's not just exercise that has this effect; musical activities, drama and art therapy also have proven benefits to mental health.

I think play is really important.

Setting aside the time to play is I believe a discipline and a form of self-care. Choosing not to feel guilty for taking this time or, to be labelled as selfish for taking time to play, is a deliberate and regular choice.

An aside is that I think women are called selfish for playing in a way that men rarely are - think golf.

I take time to do an art class every week and have done for the last 20 years. It is an outlet for my creative side. I do it just for the pleasure of it. It is very important for me that it be in an affirming, non-competitive environment. I don't hang my pictures unless I want to - I refuse to be judging of myself or be judged by others over my art.

When I am immersed in being creative, I completely forget about any of my worries and come back to my life refreshed.

- Kate, mid-50s, therapist

Play is a state of mind: Play is essentially a state of mind rather than an activity, although body movement can help us get into this state. A 'play state' implies openness to novelty and risk. It relates to the concept of 'flow' — a highly focused mental state with loss of awareness of space and time.

Play is productive: The psychological concept of flow has become huge in the professional sports world: for example, the tennis player wants to be in a state of flow where there are no thoughts of winning or losing the match which might interfere with the game. When in flow, people report being alert, in control, operating from the subconscious and working at the peak of their abilities. They're also focusing on the present, not potential future outcomes, threats or anxieties.

Play is clever: *'Play is intelligence having fun'* is a quote often attributed to Einstein (but could be someone just being playful), and whoever said it, we believe it's still true.

Go out to play in Act 3

When life gets more serious, goals, jobs and pressures close in and crowd out playtime. Because play doesn't always have

an obvious purpose is a big reason why adults stop playing —
there's no reason to make time for it. Or so we think.

> The purpose in purposeless play —
> it builds your brain.

Play is crucial for adults, especially in Act 3

Our neural pathways in adulthood and Act 3 are just as
important. As we saw in the health chapter, physical and
mental movement keeps us alive. Dancing in Act 3 is one of
the most useful kinds of play that maintains and develops
brain function as well as body fitness. Older dancers think
better.

> I have hit the right spot actually in the dance world because there is a fad now for inter-generational things where dance pieces include old people, and these are being funded. I passed the audition and am now paid to be a dancer. We toured and did two nights at The Place in London. I'm 67 and retired and I have this second little career going!
>
> – Cecil Rowe, dancer

Play is an altered state of being, it opens us up to the unexpected, which is particularly important after 50 as we encounter the unexpected less and less. On cellist Pablo Casals' 90th birthday, someone asked him why he carried on playing: 'Because I think I'm making progress.'

All work and no play makes Jill a dull girl.

There's truth in this seventeenth-century proverb for girls and boys from nought to ninety. There is a famous painting by the sixteenth-century artist Pieter Bruegel the Elder, called *Children's Games*, which depicts in extraordinary detail children of 400 years ago absorbed in 83 different games, all in the same picture. What's striking is the seriousness they bring to their game, similar to the way many adults attend to their 'more important' pursuits. Apart from the expected games of skipping, ball and chase, two of the games they are absorbed in are stirring a poo with a stick, and taking a wee. There are hours of pointless pleasure and play to be had in almost everything, as all kids know – something which adults could relearn in Act 3.

Play builds community

If you move to a new place and want to make friends locally, what better way than to do some playing with your neighbours. Invite them round for something purposeless. What activity would you choose?

> You can discover more about a person in an hour of play than in a year of conversation.
>
> – Anonymous

In Act 3, start behaving like you

The greatest gift of Act 3 is more time. When you have time to yourself, what do you do? And do you *really* do it for yourself? Some people find it much easier than others to give themselves permission to pursue hobbies, pastimes and leisure activities – stuff that's not about duty, earning money or other people's agendas.

> You owe it to yourself to be you.
> If not now then when?
>
> – Unknown

Play stops time

 Think about a time when you did something and time stood still, or didn't exist. Now get your journal out and note down:

- What were you doing?
- When did you last do it?
- On a scale of 1–10, how much fun was it?
- What would it be like to do it again?
- When would you like to do it?
- What would stop you?

Because you're worth it

The wearisome L'Oreal advertising tag line above has been bugging us since 1973, but sometimes – in real life – you actually *are* worth it. As we pointed out earlier, play is something that kids do naturally, as if they inherently know how it benefits them. There is huge value in it for adults once we can get past the idea that play is an indulgence, or a waste of time, when we 'ought' to be doing something more 'useful'. In Act 3, now is the time, perhaps more than ever, to prioritise play while you still can.

I'd rather be fishing . . .

'I'd rather be fishing' is the message on a man's belt buckle in the US in the 1970s. You're bored. Your gaze wanders and suddenly in your mind, you're somewhere else, doing something you'd rather do. What's that thing? Follow the thought.

I'd rather be . . .

Allow yourself to be immersed in this fantasy world. If suddenly you get a 'I shouldn't . . .' or 'I ought not to think this', simply acknowledge those thoughts like a passing cloud and return to the fantasy picture.

Having acknowledged the playful part of you is good in Act 3, ask yourself what you want to do as a result.

Write it down: 'I'd like to . . .'

Say it out loud: 'I'd like to . . .'

Now write down all the other things that you'd quite like to do as well. Write down five of them.

Write down five more.

Then draw five more.

Can you manage another five? It's likely you can, if you give yourself permission.

Read the list out loud.

Change how you play and you'll change who you are.

Look back at dreams you used to hold dear

Answer these two additional questions:

- What did you always enjoy doing before life got in the way?
- What did you imagine you'd be doing by now that you haven't even started?

Make a start now.

Your goals in play

Go back to your tree. Picture your goal as the fruit at the end of the play branch. Always check that what you want and write about serves your roots (attitude, purpose, values and key relationships) as you create your goals.

Setting G.O.A.T.S. goals for play:
- Genuine
- Optimistic
- Achievable
- Timed
- Specific

Over the next 10 years, or before I die:
- What are my goals for play?
- Describe what that will be like, and what will it give me?

• What could stop me achieving this?
• What are the leaves (steps) needed to get there?
• In a year's time, what will you be proud you started now?

Write it in your journal.

Twenty years years from now, you will be more disappointed by the things you didn't do than by the ones you did do. So throw off the bowlines. Sail away from the safe harbour. Catch the trade winds in your sails.
– attributed to Mark Twain[10]

One-minute summary: Play

What long-held play fantasies do you have that you'd like to try in Act 3, especially ones which are easily accessible and not disruptive financially, physically or don't clash with your responsibilities? Remember what you've secretly always wanted to do but didn't. Why not now? Trying one or two of these things could be transformative. Because play is life-changing.

When we stop playing we start dying.
– Dr Stuart Brown[11]

Branch 3 - Home

> You buy furniture. You tell yourself, this is the last
> sofa I will ever need in my life. Buy the sofa. Then
> for a couple years you're satisfied that no matter
> what goes wrong, at least you've got your sofa
> issue handled. Then the right set of dishes. Then
> the perfect bed. The drapes. The rug. Then you're
> trapped in your lovely nest, and the things you
> used to own, now they own you.
>
> – Chuck Palahniuk, *Fight Club*[12]

Welcome home. The place where we can truly be ourselves, warts and all. In theory. The four walls where maybe we raised our children, live alongside our partners, guests or lodgers, or live there alone.

We're surrounded by our treasures; we automatically dismiss that squeaky noise made by the hot tap. We know there's always a list of things to fix and clean. We watch the seasons changing from our favourite window.

If your house could talk to you and share memories, what would it say?

What is your home *for* in Act 3? Somebody asked us that question, and it took us several hours to answer it.

Our own story of home in Act 3 is unusual. We were lucky, and, frankly, crazy enough to embark on the enormous and demanding project of building our own eco home fit for purpose as we age. A once-in-a-lifetime chance to build a home to see us out – in a box. Well, in theory anyway.

When you're given the chance, as we were, in your late 50s to design every centimetre of where you live, it carries with it a huge weight of getting it right. And although we got a few things wrong, we love living here, and we still feel so lucky we could do this.

But it took a huge leap of faith, a lot of patience and 7 years of waiting and writing letters before the right plot came up. It means we had to think hard about our potential needs as we decline: living on one floor, doors and hallways wide enough for wheelchairs or Zimmer frames, a big wet room for easy showering.

'That's where Judy will hose me down when I'm an old man,' says Adrian to visitors. Or it could end up being the other way round . . .

Your four walls – fit for purpose?

Where do you live now? Do you love it and want to live there for the rest of your life if you can?

What might you need as you grow older in your home?

The three main areas you need to think about are:

1. Does the home itself work well enough for a person with known and unknown ageing needs? The fabric of the building, the stairs, the garden, the maintenance? The running costs?
2. What's on the doorstep? When you can't drive or cycle any more, how will you get out and do stuff and buy things? Online shopping is great, but a trip to the local shops has the bonus of human contact and stretching your legs.
3. Who's coming round? (See the section on friends.) Are you hoping to have a houseful of family and friends visiting? Perhaps you'll let that spare room to someone who needs a home? At what point might you say 'I no longer

need all those shed tools,' or 'I'm beyond cooking Christmas dinner for 12'?

> *Don't make it too easy for people to come and stay. Stick with the proverb 'Fish and visitors smell after 3 days.'*
>
> *- Judy's dad*

Sorry, Dad, that's bollocks.

In order to answer these big questions well, put aside some time, make a favourite drink and sit in a comfy chair that helps you feel at home.

What is your home for?

 In your journal take a fresh page.

What is your home for in Act 3?

Answer this in as much detail as you can. Create a vision of you living there in the remaining decades until you are moved into a care home or death intervenes.

- What is your home for in Act 3? List your values in 5 words.
- What does it need physically?
- What facilities would you like within walking distance, or easy public transport links?
- What feelings do you want in your home?
- How do you want to offer hospitality?

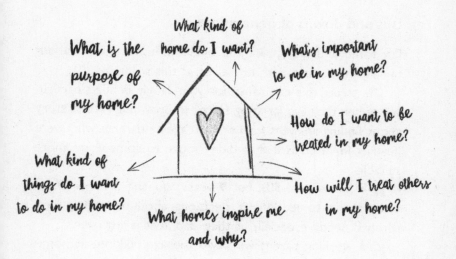

What kind of home do I want?

What is the purpose of my home?

What's important to me in my home?

How do I want to be treated in my home?

What kind of things do I want to do in my home?

How will I treat others in my home?

What homes inspire me and why?

Home is a loving base from which to fly.

Ups and downs of downsizing

In many residential streets in the UK, ours for example, there is a range of accommodation from 1-bedroom flats to 6-bedroom houses, with many smaller houses in between.

> *My partner and I sometimes think about the big family houses with just 2 people in our street, kids gone long ago. We're mindful of the heartache caused by leaving it too late to move, and being able to enjoy a new lease of life somewhere much more fit for purpose as we age.*
>
> *- David*

Ups and downs of generations

For some of us in Act 3, the problem of home is more about our ageing parents than ourselves, at this point.

The stress this can cause for your family is huge, particularly when they live far away. Here's Jo Browning Wroe's story about finding answers for her own ageing parents who were heading for a crisis if they didn't move to somewhere more suitable.

Jo is in her mid-50s, but 9 years ago, she and her sister were facing some difficult decisions about managing their parents' needs, especially as their dad kept falling over.

Jo, a working parent with two teenage children at home, lived a 2-hour drive away. Her sister lived near their parents, but was getting phone calls at all hours of the day and night.

My parents at that point would have been mid-70s, and my father's mobility, in particular, was a real problem. He was falling, and having real difficulty getting up and down stairs. My sister and I were aware at the time that a new residential retirement village was being built and we thought it looked good. So we put them on the waiting list. We said we were going to do it, and they didn't seem that keen. But we said, 'There's no harm, we'll go to the Open Day, and then see.' Just before the Open Day, my dad said, 'I don't think I want to go,' but we said, 'Just come, come and see.'

They did such a good job on that Open Day. They had residents from another retirement village, who came and talked about their active lives, and how it was NOT about sitting in a corner on a chair with a plastic cover. It was about being able to be more active. They took people on holiday, rock climbing with all sorts of infirmities. There's clubs, choirs, wood-working, gardening, a sewing room. Equally, if you just wanted to be in your own flat and shut the door that was fine too. And the people from this other place just seemed so with it, so active, that on the spot my dad said, 'I'm sold!' The apartments were beautiful, brand new, like a posh hotel really. My dad actually said, 'I never thought I would be able to live somewhere like this.' We were just so glad that we had said, 'Come on, let's just go,' because if we hadn't, at that point, it would have got really, really difficult with his falls.

There was constant stress on Mum - we thought she had Alzheimer's; she seemed very forgetful, jittery and anxious. But once they had moved, that subsided so much, and we think that was the stress of living with Dad who was like a time bomb, having all these accidents.

They have lived there for 9 years now, although Dad has since died. There is so much on offer for them, as well as all their practical needs taken care of. The activities and trips out are endless. In fact for Mum's first birthday there, Dad bought her a pair of walking boots because she had joined the ramblers club - something I never imagined she would do.

When one of a couple dies in their retirement village, the lovely thing is there isn't a taboo. People will talk about it, and remember the person, and say how sorry they are. It's a strange thing in a way, because they all know they're on the edge of this, so when someone does die, there is just support and warmth, and a lot of remembering and referencing.

Mum is still there, and she's so happy. I go and see her and take her out for lunch, but it's just such peace of mind knowing she's happy and safe. The thing I love most is this duality of having her own front door, and her lovely balcony that looks out over the trees. And yet, she steps out of her door and there is a community. It's such a great thing, the community is there and there is no pressure to be part of it, but if you need it, it's there.

I know these retirement villages are not available to everyone. But I do think having elderly parents in a home that's not safe for them is unbearable for everybody, and it's not good for them either, so you have to find some other solution.

Jo's story of having to deal with elderly parents, or someone you have some responsibility for, points towards a big theme throughout this book: *Why wait for the crisis?*

We appreciate how hard it is if you are nowhere near making progress with this – we have been there with Judy's mum who was fiercely resistant to moving into a care home. Her Alzheimer's had worsened to the point where having one carer looking after her at home was too difficult. Carers would frequently be replaced, and one night, yet another new carer had not realised how to double lock the front door properly, so in the middle of the night, Judy's mum got up and let herself out of the flat. She was found by police at 3 a.m. in a nearby park in her nightdress with one slipper. From that point on, we knew we needed the extra security of a care home. It was agony, it created huge feelings of guilt, but it also meant some relief that she was with other residents and staff to keep her safe, cared for and occupied.

Where else could you live?

Yet again, loneliness in Act 3 features here whether you're in a home you've had for years, or have moved somewhere new. And your loved ones worry about you. A recent survey found that one third of people questioned, worry about their parents being lonely. One third also feel guilty about not spending enough time with older relatives.

So what helps?

Long before the retirement village or the care home, it's exciting to note other creative combinations of people sharing homes and communities. The co-housing movement is on the rise. Sharing communal spaces, living areas and gardens, the option to cook and eat together, as well as having your own apartment or home are the answer for many. (See resources.)

How else could you live?

Sometimes staying put, but reworking the footprint of the home might be the answer, saving stress, time and money.

We're a fresh empty nest. It's great, yet it hurts like mad. We have always wanted our kids to be independent and leave home, but now they're gone, it's too quiet and there's always enough hot water. We've had to face our feelings, and talk about the impact on us as individuals and as a couple. And of course, in the current climate of jobs and housing costs, one of our kids is about to come back home again for a few months between jobs.

If you and your partner are finding the empty nest more challenging than you thought, can you divide up your spaces and create some independence?

Journalist Angela Neustatter, who we mentioned in Root 4 – Key Relationships, writes in her book *A Home for the Heart*[13] about how her home lost all its vitality after her children left, leaving only the space in which she and her partner would bicker. They decided they wanted to live separately, but also stay under the same roof, so they adapted their house into two semi-self-contained flats, which greatly improved their relationship.

Do something really radical

You will also remember we spoke to Phil, a PR man who decided in his early 50s to quit the treadmill of corporate life in New Zealand, and instead work for charities in Nepal and Bangladesh for a while. He and his wife sold their family home and bought two apartments instead, one to live in, one to rent out, now their children were growing up and leaving the nest.

Phil's adventurous spirit inspired a friend, as he says:

A couple of years ago, having been working away overseas, I got back in touch with a friend from my home town. I hadn't seen him for years. He's quite a buttoned-down character, everything well planned. He said, 'I've seen the things you've been doing on Facebook and I found it really inspiring.' That pulled me up, you know, and he explained a friend of his had died recently too. He and his wife had started to change the way they structured their life. They sold their house and moved into an apartment, which for them was quite a big thing. In the last year their kids had moved out. So they rented out their apartment and moved to north of Auckland and were throwing themselves into a venture with some friends, and doing some physical work and doing up an old hotel. And subsequently they bought into the business, and are doing it as equal partners. They are running it as a B & B, and as a reception venue. And this is just for a few years and maybe they'll sell it. But they'd cut themselves free, essentially, from their earlier life of jobs and having everything locked in.

What are people saying to us about moving in Act 3?

We moved 100 miles away from our home of 30 years to a much smaller home, to be in the same town as our son and his family. It's been harder than we thought. The family don't need us as much as we thought they would, and we don't know anybody else here. We really miss our old place, our neighbours and knowing where to find what we need.

> – Jonathan, engineer approaching retirement

It's fantastic being in a home that's easy to look after, cheap to run, and with just enough garden I can manage. Our old home was a never-ending list of repairs and expense which was really keeping me awake at night.

> – Jane, widow, 76

> I think wherever I move to next, is where I'll get old and doddery. I looked at one place on a hill and I thought in ten years' time this will be too steep and I won't be able to do it. Then I'll have to move into another flat.
>
> I've never understood people who want to live in a remote but beautiful place, there's a denial about what you're going to be able to do. At 61, I can still walk up and down the stairs, I see people younger than me who can't do that. I used to smoke, I'm a bit overweight, but you never know what's going to happen.
>
> – Richard

Some big stuff here. We don't want to make this branch of the tree weighted down with the negative stuff, but it's important to face it properly, which might be painful.

Act 3 home issues can hurt. Change brings up fears of the unknown. We might have to face some hard truths, maybe that our precious memory-filled home is not going to work for us as we age.

Some people love change or transition and are really energised by it, or moving house works well for them, like Jo's parents found. But for those who struggle, we have ideas for you in Chapter Eight on transition.

Move earlier

We have met and coached plenty of people whose parents have moved too late, or not at all, and it's been a huge source of misery and stress.

What helps:

- Move while you have some energy left to make new friends and build relationships with new neighbours.
- Move while you have the ability to create new everyday habits such as buying the milk, or to find the scenic routes to get anywhere compared to Acts 1 and 2, when it was more about the fastest route.
- Move knowing it can take a while to settle, you can experience feelings of shock, upset, regret and loneliness. You can also feel delighted, excited, relieved and find a whole new lease of life. As can your family who have been worrying about you.

Making plans is not everyone's cup of tea, but we believe that home is one of those Act 3 areas which works best when you take control, plan well, and who knows, maybe you'll even enjoy the ride.

Your goals in home

Go back to your tree. Picture your goal as the fruit at the end of the home branch. Always check that what you want and write about in home serves your roots (attitude, purpose, values and key relationships) as you create your goals.

Setting G.O.A.T.S. goals for your home:
- Genuine
- Optimistic
- Achievable
- Timed
- Specific

Over the next 10 years, or before I die:
- What are my goals for home?
- Describe what that will be like, and what will it give me?
- What could stop me achieving this?
- What are the leaves (steps) needed to get there?

One-minute summary: Home

Think about your home – before it's too late, it's important to have a serious audit. Ask yourself if where you live now will work for your ageing needs. Those tough questions: What will I do when I can't manage stairs? How will I look after the garden? My family live too far away for me to see them regularly – should I be closer to them? What will it cost me mentally, physically, emotionally and financially to move, or stay put? Get help answering these big questions from people who know you well, and you can trust.

Think about how else you could live. Be adventurous, while you have the energy and time to try something different. Is it a retirement village? What about co-housing? What about altering the home you have and sharing it differently? Keep adding your thoughts to your journal.

This could be your best move yet ... Just don't leave it too late.

> The ache for home lives in all of us. The safe
> place where we can go as we are,
> and not be questioned.
>
> – Maya Angelou[14]

Branch 4 - Friends

I am because we are,
and since we are,
therefore I am.
     – John Mbiti, philosopher[15]

We are aware that reading this friends branch could be very difficult for you if you're experiencing painful feelings around friends, loneliness or broken relationships. We would understand if it's too much for now, and we hope you might feel able to return to it at a later date.

Where would we be without friends?

Just think about what friends give us. A laugh, a listening ear, a mate to do stuff with. A life without friends (real ones, not cyber ones) is, well, can you imagine it?

You might have thought about some special friends, best friends even, when reading the key relationships root. In this branch, we're talking about your friends and neighbours who are just outside those special one or two friends in your tree root. We're interested in who else is in your network in Act 3 to give to and receive from. Some people include extended family here.

Old mates

By the time we hit Act 3, we share quite a lot of precious history with our old friends, if we are lucky enough to have them. People we have done the life-miles with through relationships, children, work and home. As the poet and philosopher, Ralph Waldo Emerson said:

> It is one of the blessings of old friends that you
> can afford to be stupid with them.
> – Ralph Waldo Emerson

We prefer the word vulnerable to stupid.

What about new friends?

A great gift of getting older is more time. For many, working and family commitments change, blank spaces emerge in the diary, giving us a chance to take up or resume interests, as we've discussed in the play branch. In doing so, we bump into like-minded souls who join us in a new adventure, whether on the doorstep or further afield. Here are some ways we meet people:

- That person you have started chatting to in the gym or the one who shows up in the local shop around the same time you do.
- The people who moved in up the road recently and are new to the area, so you invite them round for a drink with some neighbours.
- Or the people from all walks of life you meet through volunteering. Will it extend to a coffee and swapping numbers? You get to know these kindred spirits over the washing-up in the drop-in centre, or sorting out the bags left at the charity shop.
- The other Act 3 people you might meet who are just as bonkers as you are as you take up a seismic physical or mental challenge against the odds – you go up Mount Kilimanjaro like old goats.
- What about night school 40 years after failing that O-level? And there you find new friends – a shot in the arm for your Act 3 spirit.

List your friends

List as many of your friends as you can think of *without* going through your address book.

Go back to the circles exercise in your key relationships root. Add some more circles and put in those names from your list of friends. Keep going.

When you really can't think of anyone else, look in your address book and see who you have forgotten. We don't (usually) mean to forget people, but in Act 3, our memory is not the friend it once was.

Neighbours

We feel very fortunate to say we have many great neighbours, but it's taken nearly 20 years of living in the same street – and some work – to be able to say that. It's very common to hear nightmare stories about neighbours. The fear of what may go wrong with neighbour relationships may be what keeps many people from interacting with them – or even saying 'hello'. So nothing ever really gets off the ground. We were talking to someone who is most upset because his neighbour has started major building works in the next-door terrace house without bothering to implement a party-wall agreement.

Getting to know neighbours can take a bit of time and effort. Especially if you have moved to a new area. You might need to make the first move. Australian writer and radical community worker Dave Andrews says there are two occasions when it is much easier to meet your neighbours. One is at Christmas time, when people are feeling more up for sharing mince pies together, and the other is when you first move into the street and everyone is curious to know who you are. Dave has often seen both these ways work well with all sorts of people.

Taking on Dave's idea, most years, from the time we moved into the street, we have had a neighbours' Christmas party where all are welcome, young and old. It helps keep the neighbourly glue going all year round, and from that, friendships have formed, babysitting and dog walking have been exchanged and ladders borrowed. Outside of party mode, it's the ordinary moments of meeting in the street over the wheelie bins that have built the bonds of trust, key swapping and friendship over the years.

> You can't stay in your corner of the forest waiting for others to come to you. You have to go to them sometimes.
> – Winnie-the-Pooh,
> *The House at Pooh Corner*, A. A. Milne[16]

Throw me a lifeline

The advantage of getting to know your neighbours socially in the first instance means you're much more likely, over time, as friendships grow, to support each other when there's a problem, let alone a crisis.

> We are sitting outside your tent.

As a boy living in Zimbabwe, Adrian's family heard the phrase 'We are sitting outside your tent', when someone in the village was experiencing sadness, loss or trauma. The tradition was the locals would show compassion by sitting outside the person's home in solidarity. Waiting quietly in support.

In Act 3, you're likely to need each other more – why wait

for a crisis to go and knock on your neighbour's door? The drama of a crisis is reduced by knowing who can help in minutes – which eases the anxiety for you, and it's a relief for your loved ones, especially if they live miles away.

Geography is important

Long before the crisis (the falling over, the heart attack, the burst pipe, the lost keys), knowing your neighbours creates that sense of belonging to a wider patch worth caring about – more than just your own home – your neighbourhood. It helps extend your safe area beyond your own front gate.

Knowing your neighbours builds your community

There is plenty of data on the value of being connected to a community, especially in Act 3.

The word 'community' is not everyone's cup of tea. But lack of community, people to call on, people who care, has serious implications.

Journalist George Monbiot writes:

When isolated people who have health problems are supported by community groups and volunteers, the number of emergency admissions to hospital falls spectacularly.

Sometimes this means joining choirs or lunch clubs or exercise groups or writing workshops or men's sheds (where men make and mend things together). The point is to break a familiar cycle of misery: illness reduces people's ability to socialise, which leads in turn to isolation and loneliness, which then exacerbates illness.

The problem of loneliness

In the health trunk of the tree, we considered the major problem with our ageing population (and our young ones too) suffering from loneliness.

Those with strong social relationships had a 50% lower chance of death across the average study period (7.5 years) than those with weak connections.
– Social Relationships and Mortality Risk: A Meta-analytic Review[17] *by Julianne Holt-Lundstad, Timothy B. Smith, J. Bradley Layton*

Get to know your neighbours: start by saying hello

In the same way as we talked earlier about how managing your feelings starts with acknowledging them. If you make the first move and say hello to your neighbour, even if you have never done it before, something valuable happens when you recognise their existence.

We moved into a house on a busy road - a bus route. That summer, we had a housewarming, and invited all the neighbours and some friends. What was astonishing was the fact that one or two of the neighbours on our side had never spoken to the people living over the road in spite of the fact that they had the same age children. We could see the traffic issue was a barrier, but by simply opening our home that day, something changed, and people were happy to wave or even, shockingly, speak to each other across the street after that.

- Ben and Peggy

Be a listener

Eighty-year-old Archie lives on an estate, where he is also the primary carer for his wife who has dementia. Nevertheless, he has always believed it's important to make time to support his neighbours too — one way he does that is by listening. Even if he can't come up with any answers, listening without judgement has great value as it helps people feel understood, which in turn helps them feel more resourceful.

> *I'm pleased to be living on this council estate. A lot of the people here haven't got the desire to stir up and create a better life or even have a plan. I like to think I can be their voice, you know. If an unmarried mother with a 7-year-old daughter comes out of her house and somebody's sleeping there drugged up, she doesn't know what to do – but she knows it's not good for her, or her daughter. She knows it's not right, but she doesn't know what to do. So I just listen to her, I find that important.*

Listening is a huge part of what we do as coaches to help people feel stronger, and give them clarity to find their own solutions. See the listening skills list in the key relationships root.

Who is my neighbour?

Who are my neighbours?
How can I get to know them better?

Draw a map of your neighbourhood with your home in the middle. Mark on it the people you know.

- Who do you know by name?
- Who are you friendly with?
- What would it take to get to know them?
- Who would you call if there was a crisis?
- Who could you get to know? (It starts by saying hello.)

A dog is for life

I have spent most of my life alone. I had a very difficult childhood, and have been disabled since I was born, so I have always felt excluded. Fortunately for me I have always been content with my own company. I can spend lengthy periods alone without stress.

However, since acquiring a dog, I have made many new friends. Just chatting to people as you plod round the park each day, has helped forge new friendships. When I hurt myself recently, one dog-walking friend came to help clear up the mess, another took my dog overnight, and also took me to A & E. Today I have another dog-walker's hound with me, so he can go to hospital. We have formed quite a support group.

There are lots of opportunities to volunteer, things that don't necessarily require you to be active.

My partner – who lives elsewhere – never had a dog, but I helped her find one who is very cute who promptly found a hole in the hedge to visit the neighbours before they even vaguely knew each other. Now the dog and my partner visit and they have struck a firm friendship with her neighbours. They even dog sit when we go on holiday. Result.

– Anonymous

Your goals in friends

Go back to your tree, and then looking at your neighbourhood map, picture your goal as the fruit at the
end of the friends branch. Always check that what you
want and write about in friends serves your roots
(attitude, purpose, values and key relationships) as
you create your goals.

Setting G.O.A.T.S. goals for your friends:
- Genuine
- Optimistic
- Achievable
- Timed
- Specific

Over the next 10 years, or before I die:
- What are my goals for friends?
- Describe what that will be like, and what will it give me?
- What could stop me achieving this?
- What are the leaves (steps) needed to get there?

Example

*I want to make sure I speak to my immediate neigh-
bours at least once a week. I will invite them round each
summer. I will start by knocking on the door over the
road on Saturday, as new people have moved in.*

One-minute summary: Friends

We're getting more and more isolated in our culture, which
is very bad for us in every way, especially in Acts 3 and 4.

As we age we will need our friends and neighbours more, not less. And they need us. But unless we take the initiative in getting to know them while we can, it won't happen. But if we do, it's a win–win.

The African saying 'It takes a village to raise a child' could be rewritten to:

It takes a village to age well.

You get out what you put in: Cherish your old friends, and make new ones. Same goes for the neighbours.

You don't know the whole picture: You don't know the whole picture of what is happening in people's lives that might make them difficult or unreasonable sometimes.

You only need one or two friends: Remember, you only need one or two friends who you can be your true self with – they are probably in the key relationships root. With everyone else, be kind, be compassionate, be forgiving.

Common ground: Friends and neighbours are about trust and mutual giving and taking.

Pádraig Ó Tuama, writer, poet and former leader of Ireland's peace and reconciliation organisation, the Corrymeela Community, quotes this Irish saying: '*Mo sheasamh ort lá na choise tinne*', which translates as:

You are the place where I stand on the day when my feet are sore.[18]

Enjoy the common ground.

Branch 5 - Money

We make a living by what we get,
but we make a life by what we give.

– Anonymous

We've noticed that many people who attend our workshops have understandable concerns about paying for their old age. In this section we hope to show that an obsession with money will not serve you well in this stage of life. Instead we believe that forward planning and a renewed openness to what's fundamentally important to you is your far better bet. It links directly to attitude, purpose, values and key relationships.

Money worries

Fear and anxiety for many people get in the way of thinking clearly and helpfully. General worry and unresolved thoughts swirling in your head result in frustration, powerlessness and feeling worse. Some fear their pensions are worth peanuts, redundancy could strike or kids could need more than they think.

It is our view that many get anxious in Act 3 for these reasons.

Envy and fear

If your financial goals for Act 3 are based on unrealistic or fantasy lifestyles, you're in a bind. You fear you may not be able to attain the standard that others seem to have. To counter that fear, let's get practical right away: get your worst fears out on to the table and say hello to them, to take the power out of them — then make a plan.

Use your journal, or a large piece of paper, and just do a brain dump of all your money worries, real or feared.

We will help you sort out a plan later in this chapter.

It's about philosophy not economics:

When I became an independent flea (i.e. turned free-lance), I realised that there was a trade-off. I could sell all my waking hours and make quite a lot of money. But on the other hand I didn't have to do that. I could sell half my time and make half as much money. So then you have to say to yourself, What do I really want to do with my life? That's why I say in the end, it's a question of philosophy not of economics. You do have to say: what is my life about; how do I count success; how do I want to be remembered; what difference do I want to make in the world - oh and by the way, I need some money. But how much money and what am I going to sacrifice if I want more money?

My wife and I set strict limits on how much money because it takes up a lot of time. We try to do only things that we think are really useful; a bit of prostitution to pay for the groceries.

- Charles Handy[19]

Money is entirely roots related

It is of utmost importance to base your own financial goals at any time in your life, but especially in Act 3, on your *own* attitude, purpose, values and key relationships – the roots of your tree.

Swim against the current

Our society is very good at telling us what to buy; what level of consumption we should aspire to; what car to drive, clothes to wear, holiday to take. All this is about what others want to sell you, not what's actually good for you. As a former advertising man, Adrian is the first to admit that's what's going on. Just watch the ads on daytime TV for a few minutes, if you can bear it. You may find yourself walking to the window, flinging it open and shouting, 'Hang on! Whose life is it? This is MY life!'

Take back control of your spending and you'll be much happier. There is still wisdom in this recipe for happiness from Charles Dickens:

> Annual income twenty pounds, annual expenditure nineteen pounds nineteen and six, result; happiness.
> Annual income twenty pounds, annual expenditure twenty pounds ought and six, result; misery.
> – Mr Micawber, David Copperfield[20]

Redefine rich

The likelihood is that many people, at home and across the world, would think you are already rich, but it may not feel that way to you. Imagine taking control of spending by ignoring what other people spend, by ignoring what advertisers tell you to buy, by sleeping on a decision before making any purchases beyond housekeeping.

Property investments

Property is no longer as safe as houses. In the UK we've had a love affair with buying houses since the 1980s. And many people approaching Act 3 think 'The equity in my house will be my pension.' But take advice. Will you really be able to live on your 'investment'?

The downsizing dream trap

There are big psychological barriers to downsizing, moving to a new area and stopping work just when you're probably about to spend *much* more time in your home. Are you really prepared for this? Do you want this? What will it feel like? Check out the home branch for more detail on this.

Property assumptions around downsizing

Check your assumptions, just in case downsizing may be more difficult than you imagine. For example, will you be retired from work? Will you have paid off the mortgage? (35% by age 65 will not have) And will your children, if you have them, have left home? We've come across people who have everything worked out in minute detail, and others whose attitude is just to cross their fingers.

Your assumptions

Will you be retired from work? Yes / No
Will you have paid off your mortgage? Yes / No
Will your children have left home? Yes / No

Ditch the debt?

Right now UK consumer debt is at a 30-year high. We see lavish borrowing on cars and holidays. Personal Finance Society chief executive Keith Richards (no relation) says this is becoming unsustainable: 'Borrowing levels are at a high not seen since the late 1980s, when consumers became so mired in debt that record numbers of personal bankruptcies and home repossessions took place.' This is not the place to offer specific financial advice, as we said at the beginning of the book. We don't like having money conversations ourselves, but have found seeking professional advice has been very reassuring. There is plenty of help out there for finance issues, so please refer to the resources section at the back. Again, it's about action and planning, not denial.

Your kind of rich

If your kind of rich is having the ability to spend time with friends and family, to sleep at night without worry, to be occupied with something meaningful – paid or not – to experience love and respect, to do some of the things you love, to be active, in reasonable health and growing as a person, then you're our kind of rich.

> Not everything that can be counted counts, and
> not everything that counts can be counted.
> – William Bruce Cameron[21]

The truth will set you free

Make a spreadsheet or list of average monthly outgoings. Every tiny thing, even that cup of coffee you bought this morning.
   Ask yourself of each item:

Do I use this?
Do I need this?
Does it give me joy?

Then cancel everything you can. Put the money saved towards paying off debt and if you've done that, put it into savings.
   Even if you try really hard to cut costs, sometimes it isn't

enough. That could be just the time to seek professional advice on managing your money.

Use a jam-jar bank

This maybe comically old fashioned, but it works. A couple we know going through hard financial times put a jam jar on the mantelpiece. They put in it a fixed sum every week out of which they would pay all their expenses – in cash. Everything else went to paying off debt. When you see the actual cash going out on groceries and utilities, it is far more real to you. It really helped them get back to a good footing financially. There are much more modern versions of the jam jar – bank apps, for example – to help you be very controlled over your spending, but the principle is still the same.

Include others

Your financial adviser or Citizens Advice Bureau will run you through all this, but why not organise a time to share your plans with your children, parents, other family or friends? (Read about Nina's family who did that in Chapter Nine on death.)

Do a financial favour

Do you have a financial plan in place for Act 3 and Act 4? If so, when did you last review it? Perhaps your parents are still alive – it's important to know how to contact their financial adviser, solicitor or accountant, if they have one. See Chapter Nine on death for will making and lasting power of attorney.

What's your filing system?

Do you have a record of assets and important documents and where they are held?

Create a folder, in it, make a list of bank, pension and investment accounts and the account numbers. Who needs to know your passwords before you can't remember them, or can't remember where you wrote them down?

Make a note of this, too. There are digital ways to do this, but as a friend of ours said, 'Write it on paper and file it on your shelf as burglars don't want to steal paper.'

A classic error

Adam Bullmore's father was fairly successful in business in London and liked to race classic cars. He was known to keep them in lock-up garages scattered around town. Sadly, he neglected to write down their locations, so after his unexpected death, no one knew where these valuable cars were. They were all lost.

Unequal can be fair

When it comes to inheritance, we know of at least two families who agreed an unequal inheritance in favour of one child. But they took care to do this after discussion and agreement with all the siblings, all of whom were adults. We've found people can be surprisingly generous and open to creative ideas if you approach them sensitively.

Fair is not always equal

Long before they died, Maggie's parents had already spoken to her two siblings, agreed with them and written into their will that Maggie would inherit the majority of their estate — which was their house — when they died. Everyone was happy with that.

Her parents were in their mid-80s when they died within a year of each other and she in her early 50s.

Maggie says:

I became more aware of my own mortality and the relative shortness of the years I had left. I wanted to make sure I used the time well, so applied to train as a music therapist. I was also thinking this might be a good way to continue earning a living later on in life, as I knew I wouldn't be able to make ends meet on a small pension. With the agreement of my brother and sister, my parents had left me enough money to pay off my mortgage and other housing loans, and so with some of the balance I was able to fund music therapy training.

Money, money, money

Earlier we asked you to write down all your fears around money.

While you've still time in Act 3, reflect on the issue of money for what would be most positive for you to work on.

Choose one of the worries you wrote down, that if you could make some progress on, would be the most beneficial for you, and make you feel good. It's important to pay attention to your roots. Below are questions to help you do that, with some example answers.

Is your attitude to money really serving you now?: Yes, now I have taken some positive steps to get on top of my finances, instead of being overwhelmed by them.

How will money help you achieve your purpose in Act 3?: One of my purposes is to be generous, so managing my money properly will mean I can do that.

What new action will you take?: I've heard there is a great app for money management which I will download on Saturday.

Your values around money: For example, if your values are to live within your means, a sentence could be: *I will set annual budgets across all the areas that are necessities. Then I will use anything left over for leisure and charity.*

What new action will you take?: I will put in the diary to review my finances in the third week of each month.

What role does money take in strengthening your key relationships?: It means my adult children don't need to worry about my finances.

What new action will you take?: I will arrange a video call with my adult children and follow up with an email to let them know what my financial plans are.

Your goals in money

Go back to your tree. Taking your answers to the above questions into account, create your fruit on the money branch of your tree. Always check that what you want and write about in money serves your roots (attitude, purpose, values and key relationships) as you create your goals.

Setting G.O.A.T.S. goals for your money:
- Genuine
- Optimistic
- Achievable
- Timed
- Specific

Over the next 10 years, or before I die:
- What are my goals for money?
- Describe what that will be like, and what will it give me?
- What could stop me achieving this?
- What are the leaves (steps) needed to get there?

One-minute summary: Money

Recognise your concerns over money – *do not ignore them.* Ask for help.

Reconsider your approach to money, particularly your spending and saving, and integrate this with your roots: attitude, purpose, values and key relationships. Do this while you still can. Challenge and change your spending behaviour if you need to, and don't worry what anyone else thinks. Aim low.

> The secret to happiness is low expectations.
> – Barry Schwartz, psychologist[22]

Branch 6 – World

Be the change you wish to see in the world.
— Arleen Lorrance (précis)[23]

Did Ghandi say that? Not exactly, his grandson Arun Ghandi summarised what he actually said, 'We but mirror the world. All the tendencies present in the outer world are to be found in the world of our body. If we could change ourselves, the tendencies in the world would also change. As a man changes his own nature, so  does the attitude of the world change towards him. This is the divine mystery supreme. A wonderful thing it is and the source of our happiness. We need not wait to see what others do.'

Planet Earth is a wonderful and worrying place to grow old in. The state of the world we live in is a concern that crops up regularly in our Act 3 workshops. Some people despair at the political, social and environmental mess we're in now, let alone what future generations will inherit.

Watching the news before bedtime is not a great way to get a good night's sleep if it sparks anxiety, especially about things you have little or no control over. Let alone if it's fake news (which is deliberately written to provoke you and achieve as many hits and shares online as possible to make money).

While writing this, two of the most powerful men in the world, President Trump and Kim Jong-un, were meeting to try to make historic changes in removing the nuclear threat from North Korea. We remain uncertain about what Brexit will look like and how it will change the way we feel and behave towards our European neighbours. As you read this now, what is dominating the headlines?

The environmental state of our planet though is another story. Government efforts to reduce global warming, preserve wildlife and push back on pollution seem to be far too low on the agenda.

> You can live forty days without food, three days without water, eight minutes without air, but only for one second without hope.
>
> – Unknown

Oh world!

If you are worried about the environmental threat to the planet, you're right to be.

If you are concerned about political regimes and their misuse of power, you're right to be.

Those anxieties need to be acknowledged but not dominate you to the point that it makes you feel hopeless or stops you from being able to act, or you might as well be dead.

World action

What *can* we do, what power do we have to make any impact? We hope to inspire you to see what's possible, when even trying can sometimes seem overwhelming and hopeless.

In his essay 'The Star Thrower', the American writer and philosopher Loren Eiseley[24] uses a story of a boy walking along a beach covered in marooned starfish. He picks one up and throws it back in the sea. A passer-by asked, 'Why are you bothering to do that – what difference will it make?' 'Made a difference to that one,' replied the boy.

Recently, watching a news report on plastic clogging up our oceans created vivid dreams for Judy of drowning in the stuff. (Judy's dreams are another whole colourful Act 3 story. . .) In our dreams, it is normal that our anxieties surface and sometimes enlarge. As Professor Richard Vincent wrote in the health chapter, part of this at least is the brain's way of processing and filing thoughts, emotions and experiences. Many of the worries we have about our world leave us feeling powerless, hence their presence in our dreams where anything is possible, good or bad.

Global warming

May 2018 was recorded as the hottest and sunniest on record in the UK, according to the Met Office. Great for reddening up the tomato plants, terrible for our creeping concerns about climate change.

We try and do our bit for the planet, but sometimes we wonder if our recycling efforts, being careful with water or car use, is just a drop in the plastic-filled ocean.

Why bother?

Why care about the world?

Plenty of reasons – here are two:

With many more Act 3 years in good health, you have time to do something, and time to feel the benefit of doing something constructive. You'll feel better about your contribution.

Secondly, we believe we have a responsibility towards those living here after we've gone, whether you have children or not. Others will benefit.

> *Having a child goofing around keeps you hopeful, that the world stands a chance of making it through this difficult time.*
>
> *- Naomi Gryn, first-time parent, aged 51*[25]

This 'world' part of the tree could spring shoots in a number of directions and it's not all gloom and doom. In some ways, for women in particular in certain parts of the world, there has never been a better time to be alive.

We are not experts on why or how the world is the way it is. As coaches, our job is primarily to listen, to raise your awareness and to give you tools for seeking out the best answers for yourself. We're not able to explain, or give information about everything you could possibly be worrying about at the point where you are reading this. We do offer resources at the back of this book we have had first-hand experience of.

But we see in Act 3, people are increasingly concerned about world issues, and this anxiety is a terrible drain on energy which could be put to better use.

How do we deal constructively with our 'world' anxiety?: We start by facing our worries, saying them out loud and writing them down. We'll give you an exercise on that shortly. Worries about the world, and the way we treat each other, are not just global, but national and local, on our doorstep in fact, as Timothy's story shows.

I was parking my car one day on my London street of terraced houses and because of the available spaces, had to park in front of the house of my irritable next-door-but-one neighbour, which might have made it ever so slightly less direct for her to access her house. This woman in her early 80s, whom everyone in the street found difficult to get on with, flew out of her house and confronted me about my parking. Though not fond of the woman, I'd always previously been civil

. . . until that moment, when I said to her, 'Oh, just shut up, you stupid arsehole!' The neighbour was horrified and fled back into her house and wrote a five-page letter to me saying that I would never have said that to a man or I'd have got punched on the nose. Actually I would have said that to any man. I ignored the letter and forgot about the incident until a few weeks later when there was a knock at my door. It was her, and standing on the doorstep, she said, 'I can't stand this. I want to be friends with you.' I didn't know what to say, especially as she slowly leaned forward and kissed me full on the lips for a full four seconds. On hearing the ending to my story, my wife laughed, 'Well, I guess you just got punched on the nose!'

Although many people moan about behaviour in our society, and that is often the bread and butter of the media, the truth is, some people do take action, do say sorry and do make amends.

What else are we worried about?

I think we're just going to have to man up to our fears on this one. Because Botcare is going to happen; the scale of investment and scientific research going into AI is a guarantee of that. Of course, in some ways it's already here: that perky little home device which can adjust the heating, read me a book, find the car keys – or even where I parked the car.

– Sarah Dunant, 'A Point of View', BBC Radio 4[26]

Here are some more worries

Climate change: Environmental issues – pollution, endangered wildlife, sea-level change

- Population growth – by 2025, half the UK's population will be over 55; the current world population is growing by 83 million a year
- Migration issues
- Political tensions, threat to peace
- Brexit
- Values and beliefs – collapse of societal morals
- Modern life – fast paced, global, can't keep up
- Consumerism
- Technology taking over
- Techno complexity, passwords, security

So what can be done?

In November 2018, writer and campaigner, and the 'world's oldest rebel', Harry Leslie Smith died aged 95.[27] Explaining his mission to write and protest to the end, Smith said:

In 2008 the world's economies crashed. And the following year my middle son, Peter, died at the age of 50. By 2010 my grief was uncontrollable, and I knew that only way I could expiate it was through writing about my early life - in a book and also on social media. I needed to let people know that the economic and political storms coming our way - I'd seen them before.

Describing his motivation, he wrote:

I am one of the last few remaining voices left from a generation of men and women who built a better society for our children and grandchildren out of the horrors of the second world war, as well as the hunger of the Great Depression.

Sadly, that world my generation helped build on a foundation of decency and fair play is being swept away by neoliberalism and the greed of the 1%, which has brought discord around the globe. Today, the western world stands at its most dangerous juncture since the 1930s.

This kind of article can confirm our worries, as does the list above it, but what Harry did in Act 3 was to turn his grief and his concern for the world into action. He started by writing it all out, acknowledging the issues specifically, and then doing what he was able to do. You can do that too.

What are your worries?

In your journal, write or doodle all your world worries as follows:

What am I worried about for the world?
Example: A war will break out.

What is the worst that could happen?
Example: Nuclear proliferation will mean millions will die

Having written out your worst fears, take a deep breath and a fresh page, and copy out Barack Obama's words below into your journal.

> The world has never been less violent, healthier, better educated, more tolerant, with more opportunity for people, more connected than it is today.
> – Barack Obama, in a speech for the Bill and Melinda Gates Foundation[28]

What's good about the world in Act 3?

Here are a few ideas . . .

- Modern medicine
- Education – lifelong learning
- Travel opportunities
- Financial help (in countries where there is a benefit system, a state pension and free healthcare)
- Technology
- Currently, in the UK we live in peace, not war
- A better, more equal time to be a woman
- Charities to help the elderly, such as Age Concern and Silver Line
- Retirement years increasingly seen as a positive life stage

 Write or draw five things you appreciate about living in the world at this point in history. Here are five things we personally appreciate:

100 years ago, I would have died giving birth to our first child, let alone made it to old age.

It's way easier living with coeliac disease today than at any other point in history.

Being able to communicate easily with my family in New Zealand.

Having clean water.

Our children have not been conscripted into war.

AWL / AIL[29]

Making the world a better place

Let's keep our focus on gratitude rather than fear and keep creating our goals on the world branch. We opened this section with the wisdom of Mahatma Ghandi – 'Be the change you wish to see in the world.'

I'm 63 and last week I went on my first public march, along with 700,000 other people. It was very moving to see the gentle, respectful way they were making their point to the country, and to be part of that. Not sure if it'll have any effect, but maybe it will.

- David Alexander

What you can do - just a few ideas, please keep adding your own

Write to your MP
Sign petitions
Demonstrate
Switch lights off
Shower rather than bath
Switch off running taps, fix leaks

Reuse, mend and recycle as much as possible

Buy fewer new clothes

Use charity shops

Pick up litter

Switch to renewable energy suppliers, install a water meter

Insulate your house

Share your house

Eat less meat

Grow fruit and veg

Invite neighbours round

Volunteer

Get to know someone who is lonely

Walk more or use other forms of transport

Go on holiday without flying

Cycle

Car share

Buy an electric car

Help with refugees

Be wise about your news sources

The actor Dame Eileen Atkins, after appearing in the London West End, *The Height of the Storm* – a play about ageing in which she got rave reviews – wrote to us with her own advice:

Each day do:

1. Something for someone else (however small)

2. Something for yourself (a tiny treat of some kind)

3. Twenty minutes of either just sitting quietly, or meditation, or prayer, whatever is your bag -- but clear the mind.

What changes will you make?

What are the changes you would want to see?: Think about what you want for future generations, whether you have kids or not.

What could you do, to be the change?: Think of something small, you can do everyday.

Example: 'Buy a reusable coffee cup I will actually want to use, when I remember to take it with me . . .'

Think of something a bit bigger you could do weekly: Example: Keep up with world affairs by reading a weekly summary website/publication.

Think of something really big you could do in the next 3 months: Maybe, swap your car, especially if it's a diesel-belching lump, and go car-less, or car share. Could you make your next new vehicle an electric one?

Go local: When world issues feel too big, one thing you can do is get involved locally with an issue. It will be positive and make you feel much better about yourself because you've taken back some control. And it will do some good.

Once our kids had left home, it was harder to make a meal each night. I became aware that others, single people, couples, students for example, also found it a drag to cook properly for themeselves. So we started a very simple supper club at the community centre on a Monday night, just a baked potato and fillings for £2, if you can afford it. It was just a dozen of us to begin with, but now, seven years on, we regularly cook for 40 on a rota. It's only one meal taken care of, but it's much more than that. It seems many have come to rely on it for friendship as well as the food.

- Johnny, 56

Making changes injects your depressed, overwhelmed thoughts about the state of the world with some evidence that you *can* make a difference. It sounds obvious, but doing nothing means nothing changes. By changing one small thing, that helps you, helps others, helps the planet. Like that one starfish. Don't overthink it, just do it.

What is the use of living, if it be not to strive for noble causes and to make this muddled world a better place for those who will live in it after we are gone?
– Winston Churchill, 1908[30]

Big and small ideas change the world

In our local community centre, over a 150 meals are cooked by volunteers every week to provide nourishment to the elderly, the lonely, and those with mental health problems. One of the volunteers there washes and irons the tea towels. Every week, she sees it as one small yet vital action that keeps the kitchen chugging away, feeding people. Changing the world at the clean-tea-towel level is just as much needed as loud-voiced visionaries with grand ideas; it's what you're inspired by and can offer that counts.

Here's to the crazy ones. The misfits. The rebels.
The troublemakers. The round pegs in the square
holes. The ones who see things differently.
They're not fond of rules. And they have no
respect for the status quo. You can quote them,
disagree with them, glorify or vilify them. About
the only thing you can't do is ignore them.
Because they change things. They push the
human race forward. And while some may see
them as the crazy ones, we see genius. Because
the people who are crazy enough to think they
can change the world, are the ones who do.

– Apple TV commercial[31]

And here's to the quiet ones, too, who beaver away in the
background, baking the potatoes, washing the tea towels,
picking up the litter, writing to their MP or continually
switching off the lights.

Your goals in world

Go back to your tree. Picture your goal as the fruit at the
end of the world branch. Always check that what you want
and write about in world serves your roots (attitude,
purpose, values and key relationships) as you create your
goals.

Setting G.O.A.T.S. goals for your world:
- Genuine
- Optimistic
- Achievable
- Timed
- Specific

Over the next 10 years, or before I die:
- What are my goals for world?
- Describe what that will be like, and what will it give me?
- What could stop me achieving this?
- What are the leaves (steps) needed to get there?

One-minute summary: World

In schools, children are taught to be responsible citizens, and for some this sparks a lifelong commitment to activism, campaigning or being 'do-gooders' as Judy's dad used to say in one of his many moments of cynicism.

In Act 2, we're likely to be busy with work and family responsibilities, so now with the gift of more time in Act 3, what more can each one of us do to help our world? It's important to focus on what you *can* do, instead of being overwhelmed by the size of the problems.

It takes courage, it can be hard work and unpopular when you challenge societal norms or expectations. But that doesn't mean you can't do it.

Never doubt that a small group of thoughtful, committed citizens can change the world; indeed, it's the only thing that ever has.

– Margaret Mead, anthropologist[32]

Branch 7 – Your Special Branch

Your vision will become clear only
when you can look into your own heart. Who
looks outside dreams; who
looks inside awakes.

– Carl Jung[33]

There are limitations with any tool or metaphor; and though many people find our tree
useful, you may be thinking, *Meh ... it's not
working for me.*

Perhaps someone gave you this book and it's
not floating your boat. Maybe you're thinking:

I'm OK as I am, thanks
I'm not in Act 3 yet
I'm not sure what I want for my Act 3
I have some kind of itch, just not sure how to scratch it
The things here are just not touching me
I'm just feeling blank
Yes, but why am I unsatisfied?
I just feel sort of asleep to myself

Fair enough. We come across that in our coaching work from
time to time, people are different with their own ways of
seeing their stuff, or not seeing their stuff, until they are ready.
You're not weird. Give it time. Our belief is that ideas and
clarity will come when the time is right for you.

Be kind to yourself

We've asked a lot of you so far. A lot of writing. . . a lot of
thinking . . . maybe you're worn out.

As with other feelings, it's good to say these things out loud – because if it's true for you it's *truth* for you – even if you wish it wasn't. And accepting that emotion – anger, or hurt – in yourself is the first step to moving on.

So think of this special branch as one that you name for yourself – call it anything you like particular to your own life.

The principle remains the same – go back and look at your roots: your attitude, purpose, values and key relationships. How do they relate to the feelings you are experiencing? It is our belief they will provide the intelligence you need in deciding what direction to take in this branch.

Get back to your roots.

We spoke to another advertising man also called Adrian, who is at a crossroads, in terms of his work, where he lives, and his relationships. He's not alone, many people in Act 3 appreciate the advantages of living in the moment, but with an equal feeling they should make some plans.

Adrian introduced himself:

Born in Somerset, brought up in Luton, went to Manchester for the weekend 40 years ago, still there. Hey, the beer's cheap.

I'm not a planner, that annoys me about myself, I'm totally disorganised. I'm a drifter through life. If you don't get married and have kids, you're not forced to make plans. My mother tried to tell me to get my act together, bless her. But I wouldn't want to lose living in the moment. The fact that people feel they absolutely must have a career path is ludicrous really. What's wrong with people who just get on and have an ordinary life? Accepting of ordinariness, that's something I think I've done OK with my life. I enjoy knowing people who are very different. When I was a cleaner, I loved the people I worked with; a number of them were from one of the poorest parts of Manchester. When you're a cleaner, you're totally invisible; you hear all sorts!

Sometimes I can imagine leaving advertising and working in an ordinary warehouse, I'd be fine with that. Working with different people is fine. I want to carry on working. Frankly, if you live on your own, not working would be a recipe for doing what? Maybe I'd end up drinking every day. I mean I love drinking, but, I don't want to drink all the time. I've thought if I packed up working I'd get so bored.

I suppose one of the things that has been most precious to me, has been the relationship with the kids of my friends. I have a lot of experience of helping them, including when they're in trouble with stuff they can't tell their parents. One of them wrote me a letter, 'You're not a member of the family, you're more than that.' That role is one of the things I have enjoyed and treasured most. I've always been a good listener.

Stuck?

For others, like Adrian in Manchester, Act 3 is often a time when we mull over where life has taken us, and where we would like it go, and what has been most precious to us so far. Sometimes you're not ready to do that, perhaps you're a bit stuck.

If you're still stuck right now, that's fine, don't worry. Stay with the fact you feel stuck. It's our experience that accepting you're stuck is the first step to becoming unstuck. Go for a walk. Wait a while, see what comes to mind. Then, when you are ready, go back to your roots.

It might be time for you to see what your heart wants to say to you. A bit like a quiet nudge that is hard to ignore.

Listen to your heart

As you get closer to the end of your life your heart challenges you to ask:

> Who am I, apart from my history,
> and my responsibilities?

Our heart wants us to live a big, fulfilled, meaningful life. Not just repeat old patterns and reactions that diminish us.

Your goals in your special branch

Go back to your tree. Picture your goal as the fruit at the end of the special branch. Always check that what you want and write about in the special branch serves your roots (attitude, purpose, values and key relationships) as you create your goals.

Setting G.O.A.T.S. goals for your special branch:
- Genuine
- Optimistic
- Achievable
- Timed
- Specific

Over the next 10 years, or before I die:
- What are my goals for my special branch?
- Describe what that will be like, and what will it give me?
- What could stop me achieving this?
- What are the leaves (steps) needed to get there?

One-minute summary: Your Special Branch

You're not weird if you don't know yet what you want out of your Act 3. Some hover between wanting to live in the moment, yet seeing that planning ahead would be useful. Stick to the principles we've laid out, and give it time. Accept where you are. That's the starting point for getting clarity. It will come when the time is right for you.

> Let it go. Let it out.
> Let it all unravel.
> Let it free and it can be
> A path on which to travel.
> – Michael Leunig[34]

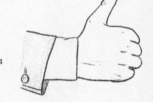

So those were the branches

Work, play, home, friends, money, world and a special branch.

In the next chapter, we'll look at ideas that will help nurture your tree, and things to watch out for that might hurt it.

Chapter Six

What Helps the Tree

For most people, a good life would be
one with a supportive family, great
friends, strong skills and knowledge,
good physical and mental health.
These are all intangible assets and it is
not surprising they are as important as
financial assets when it comes to
building a productive long life.

– Lynda Gratton and Andrew Scott,
The 100-Year Life [1]

We've tried to cram this book with ideas and actions that
will help you build a positive, resilient, life-giving Act 3.

But here are a few more essentials:

- Making plans
- Making changes
- Saying Yes and saying No

Make a plan

When our children were younger, and not in the mood to do
their homework, there were grumpy exchanges about tasks
being dashed off without planning and effort. Back then, Judy

was completing her coach training, and like all fledglings was enthusiastic and prone to quoting from coaching books. When it came to homework, (everyone cringes at the memory), she would say, 'To fail to plan is to plan to fail' in the hope this would rub off on the kids' attitude to homework. Sometimes it helped. The truth is there isn't a silver bullet when it comes to homework. Or planning.

An extraordinary example of planning is John's story:

My first wife Julia 'fought' cancer for 15 years, during which she had 4 life-or-death operations. We had plenty of opportunities to say goodbye, and eventually to talk about what would happen to me after her death.

Julia was in the hospice, depressed, when she complained to the therapist, 'When I die my husband will be off with another woman!' The therapist picked up on that, asking, 'Well, what would you want for your husband after you've died?' She decided that she would have wanted me to be happy, and to get a new partner . . . which I have.

Julia arranged it all before she died, she decided Guardian Soulmates was the best platform to find my new partner – an act of pure generosity and love. I found Julia's attitude very humbling, and it gave me permission to have a life after her death. And that's what happened – I met Ruth, my present wife, very soon after Julia died.

After the funeral I went to bereavement counselling at the hospice, and one thing that struck me over and over again was how people could not get over the shock of their partner's death. All the time they'd been visiting their partner in the hospice, they had just avoided talking about it - denial. Important things were left unsaid, like 'I love you.' Or 'Thank you for the time we did this or that,' lots of unnecessary regrets. There were people in the hospice who refused to face the truth - who'd not written a will, or considered lasting power of attorney.

Julia's funeral was great; we were determined not to make it a misery-fest, so we had a lovely funeral at her local church, with a fish and chip van outside afterwards and lots of her favourite music.

I had already started drinking far too much before she died, and after she was gone, knew I had to get a grip and get on with the rest of my life. Some might have thought I was on the rebound, but Ruth is an extraordinary person and it wasn't like that - I just struck lucky. Would it have done any good to wait 6 months, 2 years? We didn't think so. Julia had been seriously ill for 15 years.

I'm now 67 and Ruth and I are sharing a wonderful life together.

- John Lambie

Acceptance then planning

John's story is an extraordinary one of selfless love, *acceptance* and planning in desperately sad circumstances by Julia on her deathbed, which resulted in a very happy ending. It's quite hard to take in what Julia did — but the key factor for us is that she first *accepted* her own demise *and* that she wanted John to have a life after her death. This enabled her to make the plans for him that she did. This makes it one of the most remarkable and inspirational stories of planning in Act 3 we have come across.

What works?

Some people like sayings or platitudes. They cover their fridges with magnets nudging us to 'Seize the day' or 'Reach for the stars'. Cushions are scattered on sofas with sayings like 'Make Today Beautiful' or 'Love'.

Some thrive on self-help books, others run a mile. Whether it's books, websites, objects, nagging partners or parents, or your own internal compass, the best examples we have found of people having happy, fulfilling Act 3s have all been about planning.

That's why we use the Act 3 tree – to help you create a plan that will serve you best.

We met Nina, 51, who has a great story of how planning helped her, her siblings and her mum:

I'm very lucky – my 3 siblings and I are very different, but we all get on, and we're reasonably comfortable talking about certain things. Every family has its taboo topics, but Mum and Dad were very pragmatic, and logical. They had their conversations, in their early 70s, before they brought their idea to us to move to live nearer to one of us. And they moved before they had to, they were still very active and reasonably healthy. It was definitely forward planning, and them thinking, 'We won't be like this in 10 years' time.' Later, we had further constructive conversations as a family about Mum moving again after Dad died, and then about her own death and funeral wishes. We were all in tears at some point, but if you, and your siblings, are as steady as you can be, it makes the conversation much easier. So the ground was set, it wasn't like we never spoke about these things.

Making changes

Like Nina's mum, making changes well requires understanding transition and how it affects you. All this is explained further in our next chapter.

Assets

Maybe you've never thought about it, but you already have a number of assets — visible and invisible — that will feed the tree. Some are easy to recognise, some are more subtle, but arguably more important.

Visible assets:

- Right type of housing to grow old in
- Money
- Geography — access to loved ones and a local community
- Being near shops, community activities, medical care
- Good transport links
- Having interests, old and new
- Health

Invisible assets:

- Attitude
- Purpose
- Values
- Key relationships
- Health
- Confidence
- Feeling connected to family and/or community
- Religion, spirituality
- Sense of belonging
- Skills you have
- Sense of giving back
- History, experience, knowledge

The asset checker

 When you've got some time for yourself and are in a state of mind where you're happy to consider this, look at both lists of visible and invisible assets.

First, add any missing assets to either list.

Next, rank each one out of 5, to see where you need to do the work, as follows:

5. I have plenty of this
4. I have a good amount
3. I think I'm OK
2. I'm worried about this, but I've made a start
1. I am seriously worried about this

What do you notice about your scores?

What areas need the most attention?

How would you feel if you made changes in these areas?

What are the steps you need to take to move these scores up?

When will you start?

Money

Since money is one of the biggest worries in Act 3 and Act 4, we're nudging you again here as we did in the money branch.

If you're unsure if you have enough in the pot to last you out, and pay for your funeral, go and see a financial adviser. The Financial Conduct Authority will help you find one.

We know people who have left this far far too late and ended up leaving their kids to pay large inheritance tax bills, which could have been avoided with some planning.

Go to the money branch for more help.

One-minute summary: What helps the tree

Your tree is the route to creating and planning your best Act 3. It needs your time and imagination to feed it well. A healthy tree gets fed through visible and invisible assets. The visible is no more important than the invisible.

Set goals that match your roots and create plans that make you want to spring out of bed while your body still can.

Planning is everything and sometimes that means making plans for things in life that can be uncomfortable to talk about, like selling the family home or your end-of-life wishes. But everywhere we look, we see people who are relieved they have made these decisions *ahead of time*, and not left it at the mercy of a crisis.

Start those conversations much sooner than you think you

need to. If it's hard, try and find the one person who is most likely to listen to your views. It's a good idea to write out what you want to say first to get your concerns clear.

Going through life changes throws up feelings and practicalities that need attention. Please listen, give yourself room to stretch, wriggle around and experiment. Be kind to yourself. It will pass.

And sometimes you just need to pause and say 'NO.'

Or 'Maybe.'

Or 'YES.'

> Don't ask what the world needs. Ask what makes you come alive, and go do it. Because what the world needs is people who have come alive.
>
> – Howard Thurman[2]

Chapter Seven

What Hurts the Tree, Fear and Loss

As scary as living can be, stop and think
about how you will feel if on your
deathbed, you look back on your life
and conclude you never really showed
up because you were afraid.'

– James Hollis,
Finding Meaning in the Second Half of Life[1]

The metaphor of the tree is a way to help focus on what's important in Act 3 – to get priorities right. Tree roots are more important than the trunk and branches, and if we make healthy roots, the branches will  grow naturally and well. But sometimes pests attack the tree, and one of the worst pests is fear.

What hurts the tree - fear

Fear is natural: Fear is an emotional response in the animal centre of your brain to a perceived threat, causing a change in brain and organ function and behaviour. Fear can lead you to hide, to run away, freeze or lash out. Fear may arise from a confrontation, from avoiding a threat, a realisation or a discovery. Fear helps on an animal level to protect us from the tiger that may jump out of the jungle, the car that may run us over.

Fear can be the bug that eats away and kills your Act 3 tree. It can stop you making a plan for Act 3 and acting on it. If you surrender control of your life to fear, you'll miss out on living the life you could be leading. To stay as you are may be easier than making changes in the moment but leaves you walking into the future backwards.

Stand up to fear: 'Standing up to our fear is perhaps the most critical decision necessary in the governance of life, and the recovery of the soul's agenda in the second half of life,' says James Hollis in *Finding Meaning in the Second Half of Life*. The first step to overcoming fear is to acknowledge it.

> We need to say 'hello' to fear.
> – Pádraig Ó Tuama, writer, poet and mediator[2]

Vicious circles: The human mind works curiously; thoughts often circle round and round in our heads, consuming a large amount of emotional energy without ever being satisfactorily resolved. This can build fear and nothing changes or gets decided. It's stressful.

Generalised fear is bad: We often encounter a client with generalised fear; it feels like a ball of fuzz in their head, which clogs them up. It's only possible to address the fear once it is untangled and the fear made specific. We get the client to write down a list of actual concerns – all of them.

Set aside some time to have on your own when you're ready to write about and think about your fears, and consider the following:

Check your fears: Go back to what you wrote about fears in the world branch.

Add to that list all the things you most fear.

Add anything playing on your mind – your list could be 10, 20, 50 or 100 things.

List them all.

> I have seen people die and I have seen their deathbed be a place of the most tragic, lonesome, forsaken regret. People who never lived the life that they desired. Postponed it. Allowed themselves to be beset and contained by other people's expectations, and their own anxieties and uncertainties. And always were waiting for a future time to enter their lives and inhabit them, and never did. And suddenly it was the evening of their death and their sad, lonesome eyes looked back on a life they had squandered.
> – John O'Donohue, poet, ex-priest[3]

Speak your fears out loud: Having made your list, and in a room with the door closed or on a solo walk in a private place, speak your fears out loud from your list. For example, 'Yes, I'm afraid of stopping work . . .' or 'I'm afraid of growing old . . .' or 'I'm afraid of being alone . . .' or whatever you have written down.

Say them all. Speak your fears out loud.

Saying hello – conquer fear: Naming your fears and greeting them helps you take back charge as Susan Jeffers says in her bestseller *Feel the Fear and Do It Anyway*. You take back the power from those fears. It begins to return power to you.

Don't let fear prevent making a vision and goals for Act 3 and acting out a new beginning. 'Beginnings are strange things. People want them to happen but fear them at the same time,' says William Bridges in *Transitions: Making Sense of Life's Changes*.

Fear, feeling or action?: You may think all this is rather overstated, and fair enough — but what you feel is what you feel. It still follows that positive outcomes begin with action. And when you've completed the action, you feel different. Then you can raise your ambition. Step by step.

> It is easier to act your way into a new way of feeling than feel your way into a new way of acting.
> – Harry Stack Sullivan, psychoanalyst[4]

Action: *'I'd not ridden my bike for a year after falling off, but I tried a cycle ride to a pub.'*
Reaction: *'My partner said well done, I actually enjoyed it and had a nice lunch.'*
Mind: *'It gave me a confidence boost.'*
Thought: *'Let's do it again next week.'*

Action brings new reactions that change the state of your mind. This new state of mind creates new thoughts, which will create new actions. So the positive cycle continues and intensifies.

Eliminate the negative: Throughout this book, we emphasise the value of gratitude — the AWL / AIL (aren't we/I lucky) and how it can turn round your thinking and action.

And it is probably why the 1944 hit song 'You got to accentuate the positive. Eliminate the negative' had such resonance during a dark period of history.

Bring it back to a simple place: Motivational thoughts work in all sorts of situations and have been used by sports people the world over. In the 1975 men's Wimbledon tennis final, Arthur Ashe read private messages which he kept in his racket bag. His opponent, Jimmy Connors, tucked notes from his late grand-mother into his right sock. The idea is to bring yourself back to a simple, more productive place. Otherwise the athlete might be thinking: 'If I win, I make £50,000 and get to the second round and if I do that I get on the tour and get a contract and a sponsor...' and his or her mind goes at 100 mph and it prevents the athlete playing to their potential. This stops all of that.

One-minute summary: Fear

What is being human without the ability to act? Fear and negative thoughts can creep in and be very very destructive.

Confront fear. Act.

Regain your power while you still can. If necessary, seek professional help.

> If there is anything worth fearing in the world, it is living in such a way that gives one cause for regret in the end.
> – A. C. Grayling, philosopher[5]

What hurts the tree – loss

> If you know about loss, you know about life.
> – Julia Samuel, psychotherapist[6]

The tree which represents your life in Act 3 is bound to suffer loss – death is the ultimate loss. But even while we live in good health, we still experience loss on all sides from our waistlines to our memories.

£5 is equal to £10

Humans are programmed to avoid loss. Scientists have found we have a much bigger aversion to losing £5 than pleasure in finding £5. Research by psychologists Amos Tversky and Daniel Kahneman[7] shows we'd have to find £10 to equal out the pain of losing £5.

We are very tuned to avoiding loss. So, what's the art of dealing with it?

Everything to lose

Let's face it, we have everything to lose — but let's just start with eyesight . . .

> *I'm using a hotel shower that I'm not familiar with, naked, wet and without my reading glasses, trying to read the microscopic writing on the bottles - is that the shower gel, the shampoo, or the conditioner bottle? I've done it again - I'm in the shower without sorting this out beforehand with glasses on. Why do manufacturers make everything unreadable for people who need glasses?*
>
> *- Andrew, 64*

It's the same in the supermarket, squinting at microscopic ingredients lists on food packaging: trying to reduce salt, sugar and fat is enough of a challenge, let alone avoiding a serious error with food allergies.

Fading eyesight is a real loss. And that's before you lose your glasses.

Act 3 moments

It's not just your glasses – it's that creeping realisation that something you once enjoyed or found straightforward has gone.

> I used to love parties with lots of friends talking, laughing, music, dancing, but now I find noisy rooms very difficult. I can't hear as well, I get tired shouting and want to sit down in a quiet corner and talk properly. Or I just wonder, 'Why am I here?'
>
> In my 20s and 30s, I'd look at my watch and think, 'Oh good, it's only midnight. The night is young.' Now I see it's ten-thirty and think, 'How soon can we leave?'
>
> – Nancy, 55

As well as enjoyment, you notice you've lost something you once considered automatic, a skill even. And it's upsetting. It bashes your confidence.

If we're in a good mood, we might roll our eyes and mutter 'Act 3', which in our house is short for 'I'm having an Act 3 moment.'

But sometimes, noticing what we're losing feels more significant.

Loss from the menopause

In our Act 3 workshops, we ask men and women, in separate groups, to identify all the pluses and minuses of life in Act 3. Almost without fail, the menopause and its effects, from loss of sleep to waistlines, confidence and libido comes up, and not just on the women's lists.

Angela wrote to us about her experience of the menopause:

To half the population it probably means nothing. I'm talking about menopause: the stage of a woman's life when, apart from the extreme discomfort of hot flushes and other debilitating symptoms, having children becomes no longer possible. That stage when the body's ability to create new life shrivels and dies; when women have often been dismissed as being 'silly' or 'overemotional'.

The sense of this particular loss is beyond description, even for someone who's had children. And if you've never had any children at all - like me - it felt like being in a dark, empty house echoing with lost dreams, lost potential, lost lives.

I came face to face with all this pain one evening 19 years ago, aged 47. I was angry, bewildered and hurt, but I didn't want to be self-pitying. I wanted to try and face reality. There were, and are, no answers. I needed to find a way of living with the unsettling mystery that life is.

Nineteen years later, the hot flushes continue, as does the mystery.

- Angela, 66

There is more on the menopause in the health chapter, but if it is something that is literally keeping you awake at night, please seek professional help.

Potential losses in Act 3

Take a look at the word cloud below.
   List your own Act 3 losses.

OPTIMISM sex Hair DIRECTION drive
Partner FRIENDS hearing Resilience
ENERGY MEMORY CHILDREN
mobility Enthusiasm DOG Identity
KEYS Confidence Waistline Parent
Purpose Glasses

Given the huge potential list of losses at this time of life, what's the way to cope?

Retirement story:

I retired on a Friday. On Monday I had lost my world: I wasn't at work, and I wasn't on holiday. I was at home – but I felt I was dangling over the sea, disconnected from the solid and familiar ground where my status, routine and friends had grown for years. Now I was to start as a novice in someone else's daily domain – my wife's. Odd. I was in a happy home, but without any qualifications in domestic logic or management . . .

> *Landing in a different place - weaving my busy post-retirement plans into a web of homely happenings, managing others' expectations of my 'freedom', learning to change gear and building other connections took several years. The journey was eased by real conversation, prayer, agreed boundaries, looking out over big spaces, letting creativity have its way - and more conversation. It's a great place to be now.*
>
> *- Sam Wilkes*

Sam's experience is a very common one, particularly amongst people who have been in a very set role for a long time. It's linked to transitioning well, more of which will come in the next chapter.

Take loss seriously

Taking decline and loss seriously doesn't mean you're giving in to old age. It means you're being real, it means you can make a plan.

Elisabeth, who needed her reading glasses on her at all times in her 70s, refused to own up to her declining eyesight by wearing her specs on a cord around her neck – which she really needed to – instead forgetting where they were. She also thought the cord might be mistaken for a hearing aid. It was vanity really, she thought people would think this made her look old and less capable, and treat her differently.

Grief

Recently, Judy met up with her mum's bridesmaid, a sprightly lady named Jenny in her late 80s.

She confessed to Judy she's unlikely to make any more trips from England to her homeland of New Zealand. Since her last visit, just a few years ago, 6 friends have died there. 'It only leaves my sister to stay with, and she's told me she's too old for visitors now.' But she doesn't have to fly to New Zealand to be faced with death amongst friends – it's just as prevalent in her circle of UK friends.

Jenny is grieving the loss of her old friends, and missing being able to go home to stay with them in New Zealand.

In spite of the above, Jenny's great at keeping herself busy volunteering in a charity shop, reading and gardening.

It seems from those who have lived with loss, it helps to zoom out and get things in perspective, along with paying attention to what you're grateful for.

I concentrate on what I can do, not what I can't.
Others have said I have helped them;
there is only one today.
– Wendy Mitchell, blogger about Alzheimer's and
author of *Somebody I Used to Know*[8]

Dealing with the unexpected

Martin and Denise, in their early 60s, have 4 adult children and several grandchildren. Their lives and retirement plans turned upside down when they took over full-time care of 2 small grandchildren after their eldest son became seriously unwell:

We had two lodgers and one left so we didn't replace him, so suddenly we had a spare bedroom which became the grandchildren's. I can remember the night, some months after the children arrived, we were putting the kids to bed. I said to Jasmine, 'You know this is your home now, don't you?' She said, 'I do now, Grandad' – which is kind of wonderful. And awful.

We both reduced our work hours but we were spending a lot more money – it was costing us an extra thousand pounds a month – but surprising cheques arrived from friends, people in our church, people we hardly knew.

But the idea of retirement and when that might be, went out the window. The most difficult thing, I suppose, was uncertainty. Though we didn't want to project into the future, I was thinking, 'I'm going to be 75 by the time they're 18. OK. So be it.'

We were fortunate to have such support. We've had family therapy which was quite useful because we needed to process what was happening to us. The things that really helped us though, that stood us in good stead, were already in place – plus how significant and precious were our other 3 adult children and what they did for us. It would be difficult to give advice to someone who'd just landed in a situation like this, because it's too late then – we already had stuff in the 'bank': friends, community, spare room, enough money, we were both able to step back a little from work – not everybody can do that, can they? We only appreciated how lucky we were when we were in crisis management and all the help kicked in.

But in a community you hear other people's stories – often awful – and you think, 'Wow, their situation is tough. Our problem is not as big as his or her problem.'

Perspective can help – big time. Our community

were very supportive because they weren't always asking, 'How is it this week?' In terms of perspective, taking on two small kids in Act 3 isn't the most difficult thing in the world – it's not an awful thing is it?

I'm not sure if there is a silver lining – we already appreciated being grandparents, and that was only amplified and underlined. The bond between us and the grandchildren was wonderful and deep – such a counterpoint to the upside-downness of our lives. I already knew our community was great – and then we experienced it.

Someone I don't know well asked, 'Does the community know?' I said, 'Yes, they know the children are living with us.' And she said, 'Well, people can be so judgemental and disappointing.' And I told her a few stories and she was doing an impression of a goldfish. 'Oh, I've never heard of anything like that. That's just incredible.' It was incredible. And I don't know if that's a silver lining but I just felt . . . well, pride is the wrong word, but . . . I just thought, 'This place is amazing!'

We recognise that Martin and Denise's story is an extreme example of the unexpected which crashed into their Act 3. But what we take out of it is that however unexpected a loss is, it is possible to live through it and come out the other side – possibly in a better place. Holding on to perspective, and to their purpose and values, certainly helped them cope with their loss of freedom and retirement plans. After the initial shock subsided, they were able to recognise a deep sense of gratitude for their close family and community, which also made their situation more bearable.

Accentuate the positive

If you choose to think about what you *can* do rather than obsessing about what you can't, you'll make better choices and outcomes for yourself and others.

> *In the winter months sometimes the last thing I feel like doing is going out for a daily walk. But I keep telling myself to stop being so grumpy, and just leave straight after lunch, before it gets dark. I know I'll come back feeling better.*
>
> *– Tom, 67*

Ideas to deal with loss

Whether it's glasses, map reading, a much-loved pet or a family member, taking control of loss will come by taking practical action.

Pay attention to what you can do. What you can change and when you will change it.

Get outside

Do regular exercise: Walk. Stretch. Check out our health ideas on eating and sleeping too.

Engage

Make time for creativity: Write. Paint. Draw. Dance. Sing. Make music. Listen to music. Cook. Bake. Have a stiff drink. Or don't have a stiff drink – have a cup of tea instead.

Connect

Phone a friend, or someone who knows how to listen. Put something in the diary which involves someone else.

See the funny side

Keep laughing. Read something, listen to or watch programmes that make you chuckle.

Bobby Henline became a stand-up comedian after experiencing third-degree burns to his face in the Iraq war when his vehicle containing five men was hit by an IED, killing all but him. Now badly disfigured, he bills himself 'The Well Done Comedian', and happily explains how, despite his terrible injuries, it was though humour and acceptance of his reality that he experienced healing to his psyche.

Accept yourself now

Accept yourself how you are now, but stretch yourself also. We go through denial that we need glasses round our neck, frustration that it might make us look old. None of that is as bad as not being able to see.

Get glasses. Or better glasses. Put your glasses on a thing around your neck. Now, what's the plan for your keys? Anything else?

> *I have more aches than I had, so it may take me longer than when I was younger. But it doesn't stop me doing things. Mo Farah will run the marathon quicker than me, but we both can finish. It's something we have in common.*
>
> *- Neil, 56*

Debunk the myths about ageing

They focus on what you may have lost. Ignore the ads that try and flog you something to stave off the wrinkles, find the perfect partner or have the body of an athlete. Like writer and poet Rhian Roberts[9], we're pro-ageing.

Still Here

What is this anti-ageing nonsense?
This anti-wrinkle potion peddling rubbish?
How can one take a stance against time?

All those lost moments
Flummoxed by lined up promises,
Seriously considering the retinol and retinox,
The collagen and smollagen,
Shelves collapsing under the weight of so much
   buttery piffle.
Let those words spin free and be themselves again.

Me?
I'm pro-ageing actually.
Glad to be here,
Still around;
Crinkling my eyes at his daft stories.
I'm all for it,
Everyone should do it.
Now take your air-brushed lying mouth,
And sod off.

Check your losses

Earlier you listed your losses in Act 3. Go back to that list, and see if you want to add or remove anything, real or imagined.

Next, write how that loss makes you feel.

Next, write beside each loss, what the gain could be. For example:

Loss of waistline: Makes me feel sluggish, podgy, irritated.

Gains: I will accept the truth, but not let it get the better of me. I'll review my eating and exercising habits this weekend.

Loss of memory: Sometimes I forget I was supposed to be meeting a friend.

Gains: Sometimes I forget I was supposed to be meeting a friend I find difficult.

> Age is an issue of mind over matter.
> If you don't mind, it doesn't matter.
> – Anonymous

Dementia - a double loss

Dementia is one of the greatest fears for people. As you've read, it deeply affected our lives when Judy's mum was diagnosed with Alzheimer's and the 9 years of gradual loss – which felt like an extended death – were awful. One thing that hugely helped was Oliver James' book *Contented Dementia*, which gave the family practical ideas, such as:

Don't ask questions: Say 'I think I feel like a cup of tea' instead of 'Would you like a cup of tea?'

Stay with their agenda: Agree with their fantasies. If they say, 'We're flying to Spain this afternoon', don't say, 'No we're not!', say 'Ohh, that sounds nice. I love the sun.'

Avoid arguments and contradictions: If they're fixated on cards get several packs from a charity shop, instead of arguing with them, 'You don't like cards, you like Scrabble.'

Recently a photo went viral on Twitter – words of reassurance left on a whiteboard for an elderly woman with dementia by her daughter.

I'm finding being a full-time carer for Jennifer is cruel. Alzheimer's is cruel. I thought I knew something about it, but I'm realising I know nothing. It's a big learning curve. You have fears (voice cracks) . . . I'm not going to be able to do it and she'll finish up in a home. So that's the learning curve now, to be a good carer, and not lose the identity of a husband – it's very easy to do that.

– Archie, 80, carer

Living with dementia

We were inspired hearing about Wendy Mitchell (quoted earlier) who was diagnosed with early-onset Alzheimer's at age 58. She wrote a blog about her experience to record all her thoughts before they were lost.

Here's what Wendy Mitchell said in an interview on BBC Radio 4:

I can type as though dementia never entered my world, as that part of my brain has not yet been affected, but that often works against me as people question my diagnosis.

People think of dementia as an end stage but there is a middle. I started my blog to help people see. Friends were afraid and stayed away. You lose friends through dementia, but you also make friends.

I'm losing the old me and discovering the new me. The thing is don't panic. When the fog comes, stand and wait for the fog to clear. I looked out of the window the other day and thought my shed had disappeared

- I now have a 30-minute rule, then I check again - my shed was still there.

My new self remembers how people make me feel. I love poetry and short stories and finding a different way to enjoy things. I don't answer the phone, I don't feel hunger any more, I don't cook, but I do baking for the elderly.

Closed doors are a problem - I can't remember what's on the other side. So I have photos stuck on cupboards so I know what's inside.

I concentrate on what I can do not what I can't. Others have said I've helped them. There is only one today.

Wendy's book *Somebody I Used to Know* based on her blog has become a bestseller.

One-minute summary: Loss

In Act 3, forms of loss happen to everyone, yet we are very good at avoiding them and even concealing them.

By now you will have experienced loss already, to some degree, small or large. Our culture sells us the idea we can have everything we dream of with no loss or disappointment. The truth is we'll lose just about everything one day, so getting ahead of the curve and managing our attitudes to loss — getting things in a positive perspective — is crucial. If we allow ourselves to be overwhelmed by loss for too long, we can get stuck. Unsticking is done by creating positive actions that help take back control, so the negative feelings don't dominate.

> When you lose something it leaves a space
> for something else.

Chapter Eight

Accept Transition

Before you can begin something new, you have to end what used to be.
– William Bridges, *Managing Transitions*[1]

Some people might summarise all of the changes we undergo in Act 3 as 'dealing with transition'. In Act 3, as contexts change – work, kids, home, health, relationships – the real you might be painfully laid bare. That's transition. It can be hard dealing with all this, but understanding it will make it less hard. And sometimes – gloriously – there's a great influx of energy, even something to look forward to.

I was dreading the menopause, from talking to friends, and reading about it. But with the right hormone treatment and finding out what else I could do to help ease the symptoms, it's been nowhere near as bad as I was expecting. I have upped my exercise to keep my middle-aged spread under control, and that's given me more energy. It might sound odd, but I was actually looking forward to my hair going completely grey; just accepting it and stopping dyeing it or fretting about roots showing, and hair appointments.

- Annabel, 58

What is transition?

In *Transitions: Making Sense of Life's Changes*, William Bridges defines the difference between change and transition: 'Transition is psychological; change is situational. It is not events, but rather the inner reorientation and self-redefinition that you have to go through in order to incorporate any of those changes into your life.'

As Marc Lewis, neuroscientist, says, the real problem is the uncertainty, and that's something you just have to pass through until the lights come back on:

> Uncertainty is even more stressful than knowing something bad is definitely going to happen.
> – Marc Lewis, neuroscientist[2]

The pattern of life is a *series* of transitions from birth to childhood, adolescence and adulthood, decline and death. Yet the older we get – understandably – the more attached we get to things as they are.

Our experience of transition – saying goodbye to the old but not yet in a place where we enjoy the new – can be uncomfortable, because we're moving from one mental, emotional and sometimes physical state to another.

Fold your arms for a moment. OK, look at your right hand and note where it is. Now unfold your arms, move around a bit and refold your arms so your right hand is in the opposite position to what it just was. Was that easy or did you find yourself refolding your arms how you did before? It's not surprising, when you consider the large number of years you've done the same things, in the same places, with the same faces, that the adjustment takes some work.

Transition is a three-stage process

1. **The ending:** every transition starts with an ending. It's important to plan a good ending, if possible.
2. **The birth canal:** an in-between place where you're not where you *were* and not where you are about to be. Being in this state may involve chaos, confusion, pressure, doubt and discomfort.
3. **The new beginning:** people who make it through the birth canal can begin again, in a new way, energised, invigorated and prepared to make the change work.

Transition can be hard, yet you've done it before

Transition can be a challenge, but by the time you hit Act 3 you've done it many times before.

List in your journal all the transitions you have made in your life.

- Start with schools you went to:
- Did you cry?
- Rather be at home?
- Rather be at your old school?
- How did it make you feel?
- List the things that made an emotional impact.
- How was it leaving home?
- Starting a new job or college?
- What was the effect on you?

By Act 3 you've already done lots of this transition thing, such as moving home, choosing a job or a partner. Your challenge might be that you've not made any of these profound changes lately. Maybe it's been years or decades. You had some choice in these matters, whereas life-stage transition is coming whether you like it or not.

But you've certainly done it. And you can do it again.

The man who views the world at 50 the same as
he did at 20 has wasted 30 years of his life.
— Muhammad Ali[3]

Between 20 and 50 most women and men have changed psychologically. They have transformed and that transformation can continue. However, some people experience the impact of this more profoundly than others, especially those who are coming out of structured, corporate environments.

Patrick O'Gorman wrestled with his own Act 3 transition:

In my search for understanding I found very little written or said which gave me insight. I put that down to the fact that writers, theologians, academics, speakers, musicians, poets, never 'retire' or have to. So they don't know first-hand the pain of this transition. The best writing I found was by rugby columnists who talked about struggles on having to finish their careers. It's a huge problem of course in sport and leads to depression and suicide. So I definitely think there is a place for cogent analysis and insight to help those negotiating this new phenomenon. New, because people are living longer and baby boomers always sought new territory.

William Bridges proposes that managing transitions is really about helping people deal with fear and uncertainty — the key is to build trust and confidence in the new reality.

Spinning your wheels

The aim is not to get stuck in the birth canal. Not for long, at least.

> One does not discover new lands without consenting to lose sight of the shore for a very long time.
>
> – André Gide, writer[4]

No going back

In 2001, when we decided to move our family of five out of London, we knew that this move had to be permanent, that if we thought of it as a trial it'd be much more likely to fail. We behaved as if there was no going back. We said to each other, 'We won't know for a few years whether this has worked, and by then it'll be too late anyway.' It worked, in case you're interested, and we think our attitude helped.

Retreat is too easy when you have that option.

10 ideas on transition

I. Choice

It's an attitude thing. If you focus on dreading the change, that's what you'll get. More dread.

Reboot your focus. Say out loud, 'I can do this, it might hurt, but I'll get through it.'

2. Own up to how you feel

If *you* feel anxious about change, it's important to pay attention to it. Alternatively, it might be someone else who is doing the worrying. Does it have to become your problem too?

> *My wife is retiring; I know she's really concerned about it. It doesn't help either of us if I add to the worrying.*
>
> *– Paul, 67*

3. Feelings are not facts
Feelings come and go, but focus on the positives, and imagine what *could* be good about this change you're going to make.

> *Moving after 35 years was huge, but I just kept focusing on how much more time and energy our new place would give me as it'll be so much easier to look after than our old house.*
>
> *– Sandra, 71*

4. You can do this – you have done it before
Ask yourself, when in my life have I made changes before? What helped me change then; what would help now?

5. Stay in the moment
Worrying about the 'what ifs' is a fast way to feel overwhelmed and exhausted. Make lists if you're a list-making type and they work for you. If they don't, then don't. Stick with what will keep you calm enough today to make progress. Try writing or drawing what you've *done*, not what you need to do.

6. Ask for help
Your loved ones will probably prefer you to ask for help than have to put up with you being grumpy, bewildered and fearful about change.

> *After Dad died, Mum's ability to cope diminished quickly, but she refused any offers of help which was very tough for my siblings and me.*
>
> *- Zain, 54*

7. Look after you
Get out more. Walk round the block, watch the birds, drink water, breathe deeply, meditate, pray, dance, stop refilling your wine glass – you probably know all this ... but we all need to be reminded sometimes.

8. Just say 'No'
Some people find it hard to say no. What would be possible if you did?

9. Just say 'Yes'
Fear harms the tree, so what is really stopping you? Is it time to risk 'Yes'?

10. Just say 'Wait'
It could be that you need a pause button to help you before making a better decision or to have a better conversation.

Ageing is a normal life stage

'Anti-ageing' products are as insulting to older people as it would be to say to a child you're not allowed to play. Accepting ageing as normal, instead of fighting it, helps you stay positive and focused on what *is* possible at this life stage.

Expect the unexpected

> *Our daughter went through a terrible divorce. It was complicated, because my wife and I co-owned our house with our daughter and son-in-law, and he took us to the Supreme Court to try to get exclusive ownership of the whole property for himself. At the age of 60, facing retirement in 5 years, we had to spend our entire life savings defending the case, then borrow 250k to buy out his share, to ensure our daughter and her children had security of tenure and stability through the turmoil. To service the debt, our daughter took over most of the rooms in the house, which she lets out through Airbnb, and overnight my wife and I went from living in a 4-bedroom house to a 1-bedroom flat. To my wife's credit, she has accepted the change as necessary, has adapted with flexibility, dignity and grace and has never once complained.*
>
> *- Dave Andrews*

Though you've tried to avoid surprises, you may still be surprised by grief, anger, anxiety, sadness, disorientation or even depression.

One-minute summary: Transition

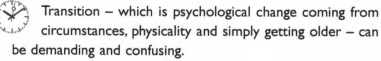 Transition – which is psychological change coming from circumstances, physicality and simply getting older – can be demanding and confusing.

The most important thing about transition is to know what you are transitioning *to*. You may not have chosen to transition at this point in time or in this way, but for reasons outside your control, here you are, making this adjustment. This is a creative process. Why not choose to see it as an opportunity to get somewhere you've always wanted to be?

Picturing clearly, honestly and in detail, and planning what you are moving *towards* is the key to success.

That's what this whole book is about.

> Having been around the block a few times . . .
> they know in their bones that negotiating a
> dramatic upheaval can be painful and
> uncomfortable at the time, and that it's often only
> when you've come out the other side that
> unforeseen positives emerge.
> – Celia Dodd,
> *Not Fade Away: How to Thrive in Retirement*[5]

Chapter Nine

Act 4 – The Art of Dying

We can't control if we'll die, but we can 'occupy death'
– Peter Saul, emergency doctor[1]

Unsurprisingly, this final chapter is difficult to write. But a book about the art of a good life in Act 3 must include a space to think about a good death. Death is still a very taboo topic in our society, which doesn't help as we go through our Act 3 years, knowing more than ever where we're heading. Our aim here is to help you die without regrets. Imagine that.

We will focus on how we respond to the prospect of our own death; why your family need you to make some decisions; and on dealing with the death of others.

Health warning

It's natural that thoughts of death generally increase with age. That doesn't mean that fear and suffering increase likewise – there's evidence to suggest that the 80+ age group generally find death less threatening than when they were younger. But, if you're finding yourself thinking about suicide or reviewing options for euthanasia, please put this book down and seek professional help. If you're feeling lonely or hopeless, tackle that first – see resources and the chapter on health.

TAKE
CARE

Death is always nearby

Throughout all of our lives, especially in the developed world, we forget that death could come at any time, to any of us. Sometimes we are aware of the near miss – the 'what ifs'. In Maggie O'Farrell's case, she wrote a bestseller, *I Am, I Am, I Am*, about her own seventeen brushes with death.

As a teenager, Adrian kicked an unexploded hand grenade out of the mud on a school trip and wondered what it would have been like if the thing had detonated.

Judy contemplated her destruction when she choked on a fly while watching the Street Child World Cup Final in Rio de Janeiro in 2014. These glimpses of death can make you feel more fully alive. Once she'd recovered from coughing up the fly, Judy hugged her children tighter than ever.

Stories, films and TV are full of death

Death is of course everywhere, and has inspired artists for millenia. Art, music, movies, books, stories are full of death. Just look at the popularity of murder mystery box sets. We even start our children early: *Sleeping Beauty* – is she asleep or dead? *Little Red Riding Hood* – 'all the better to eat you with!' and *The Tale of Peter Rabbit* – whose father was baked into a pie. Death is with us in the stories we tell from a very young age, but somehow, when it comes to our own death, or that of our loved ones, we don't want to face it.

We deny death

Judy's mother, being told of a neighbour who had recently died, simply said, 'Oh, I don't think so!' It was easier to deny that death than face the truth of it. And this was *before* she had dementia.

Act 4

Although the reality is many do die while still fit and well in Act 3, we think of Act 4 as the last chapter of our life. It might not be easy to think about, but is it time for the ultimate plan?

> In mid-winter cold, I find packing my bag for a hot, sticky climate is almost impossible. I can't think clearly about what's appropriate to put in my suitcase.
>
> Death is just as difficult to imagine. So hard to think I'll just not be here.
>
> – Jack, 64

People avoid thinking about death, let alone planning for it because:
- 'I'm frightened of it'
- 'I'm too busy'
- 'Not sure how to'
- 'I'm not a planner'
- 'That's morbid'
- 'I don't have anything to leave behind'
- 'I can't bear to think about it'
- 'I will think about death . . . but not now'
- 'I'm too young for this'
- 'I'm gonna live forever . . .'
- 'I'm up for it but my family/partner are/is resistant'

Studies show there can be a powerful perspective shift later in life when we come to understand that what we've always thought of as ownership is really just a long-term lease. The certainty of a journey's end might make better travelers of us all.

– Jeffrey Kluger,
'Why Are Old People Less Scared of Dying?'[2]

What 50-somethings think about death

Our research revealed worries are not far from the surface when it comes to this topic:

'I dread it. I can't actually believe I will cease to exist. It saddens me that I won't be there to see my children grow older too.'

'Dread, sadness, inevitability, loss, resignation, fear.'

'I don't think about it. Hope it's a long time off.'

'I've thought about this a lot more in this decade, my 50s.'

'Not worried about death but apprehensive about the dying part.'

'Been very anxious about my own death since my late 30s. If I connect emotionally with the feeling of no longer being here, I start to feel panic.'

'I'd like it to not be painful, and to be remembered.'

It's the suckiest suck that ever sucked.
– Homer Simpson[3]

Your death – what's hard to face?

This will need careful timing, and a comfortable place for you to complete the questions.

TAKE
CARE

Take some time on your own to reflect: What are your thoughts when you think about your own death?

Write or draw in your journal what comes to mind. Be free with this, don't limit or edit what you are feeling or thinking. Accept those feelings and thoughts.

In addition to our greatest, perhaps darkest, fears about death, thinking about it can also prompt gratitude and action.

Hopes surface

'I don't fear it. Generally we live too long now and I will be ready when the time comes.'

'I want to know that when I die, I have made the world a tiny bit better by being in it. As clichéd as it sounds, it feels important to leave a legacy.'

'I am slowly preparing for it, e.g. sorting files on the computer. May it be not too protracted.'

'I want my own death to be joyful – a moment of satisfaction of a life well lived and wisdom gained and purpose fulfilled, like a flower that has bloomed and withered.'

Actor Greg Wise became the full-time carer in the last months of his sister Clare's life, before she died of cancer. She wrote a blog about her experience of cancer, until she was too ill to do it, and Greg took it over.

> If you have a fear-full life, you'll have a fear-full death. If you've had a gung-ho life you'll have a gung-ho death.
> – 'You, Me and the Big C', BBC[4]

What's the art of a good death?

A good death is more likely if you pay attention to your four roots:

1. **Attitude:** your *choices* to how you approach the end: *I accept death, and I want to put my affairs in order while I can.*
2. **Purpose:** *what effect* you've had: *I've left the world a slightly better place.*
3. **Values:** *how you live: kindness matters to me – for example towards those that are caring for me.*
4. **Key relationships:** *honouring* who matters most: *I thanked important people, resolved estrangements.*

Check your obit

Very early on in this book, we asked you to face death, and write your own obituary. Go back to the obituary exercise in your journal and see if you want to add to it or rewrite it.

> *Have a good death – I think that's really important*
> *- Roger Bamber*

Roger, who was diagnosed with a particularly bad cancer in his late 50s, is now in remission, working part-time and enjoying, family, art and dog walks.

He says:

People say 'It's so unfair that you should be struck down in the prime of your life' but it just is! Shit happens, get on with it. I accepted that I was likely to die. Come on – we're all going to die, it's the one thing we know in life.

I don't do 'Why me?' It's just so negative. I actually enjoyed each day. The nurses and doctors who were looking after me were just such wonderful people – I enjoyed being with them; I still do. I only go back now once every 4 months, and they are so lovely, funny and dedicated. They have a great sense of humour – as there is around death – not just gallows humour, but you just clear all the crap. You are on the same level as everyone, it's about being honest about what we share, a human being, about to die, get on with it, and enjoy what you have left.

Have a good death – I think that's really important. There were one or two people having the chemo who were bitter, and I felt rather sorry for them, but I also thought, 'You have got this so wrong!' They were rude to the nursing staff, they were bitter to each other, and the attitude! They didn't survive – they were the ones to go first.

At my first consultation, I asked what I could do given the horrible diagnosis. We asked one of the nurses, who had been doing this a long time, what is the single thing that makes a difference to getting through this? 'Oh, attitude, definitely,' the nurse said. 'If you have a positive attitude, that means so much.'

Did I do OK?

Psychologist and parenting writer Steve Biddulph says that dads in particular on their deathbeds need an answer to the 'Did I do all right?' question.

Whether you have kids or not, everyone wants to die in peace, and that means reconciling damaged relationships.

Phone a friend?

While you're still able, is there someone you want to talk to, contact or reconnect with? Apologise to? To ask for forgiveness? To thank?

Even if they have died, it can still be very helpful to write down what you would say to them.

Write without placing limits or judgement on yourself, or thinking *'That would never work'*.

Write down:

1. Who do you have unresolved problems with?
2. What are the problems?
3. Imagine they have been resolved.
4. How would you feel then?
5. What is the first step to resolving the problem(s) with this relationship?
6. What support do you need to do this?

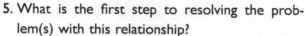

TAKE
CARE

We're aware that asking you to think and write about this stuff is tough. When we run workshops, we put breaks in to recharge. See if you need a breather now before we move on to dealing with the best ways to put your affairs in order.

Use the F-Word

It can be very hard to own up to this, but one of the things that can help the most with repairing damaged relationships is forgiveness. As Professor Richard Vincent said in Chapter Four on health, 'One of the most healing phenomena is forgiveness.'

Forgiveness is the WD-40 that smoothes the creaking hinges of our relationships – and sometimes keeps the doors from falling off altogether.
– Malcolm Doney and Martin Wroe, *LifeLines*[5]

The mess you leave behind

Whether it's a houseful of clutter, bank accounts no one knows about or simply where your will is, are you leaving a blessing or a curse for your family to sort out?

Our parents – all long dead – had almost opposite strategies. Adrian's parents pre-paid for their funerals and were on a perpetual mission of decluttering throughout most of their lives. They'd written a will and discussed it with their kids. Then they made some major adjustments to their will as a result of family conversations – several years before they died.

Judy's parents did have a will (60% of UK adults *don't*), but largely ignored their future arrangements until her dad was struck down dead with a stroke at 73 and her mum was overtaken by Alzheimer's. It took years, and many trips to the solicitor's and the local tip, to untangle their affairs.

Tidy up

The thing we say to teenagers is what we need to hear before Act 4 really kicks in. Dealing with our own mess is important and an act of love to those you leave behind.

Death decluttering

Decluttering can be enjoyable and energising because it helps you reflect on what's true and important in your life. It will help reset your priorities in the time you have left.

Start on the left

When you walk into a room and it . . . all . . . seems . . . too. . . much . . . to. . . even . . . think . . . about . . . tidying . . . up. Just start on the left. Sometimes it's overwhelming, or we tell ourselves we're no good at tidying up. Just start on the left. You'll get good at it by doing it, not by procrastinating. Just start on the left. Start with 5 minutes a day and build up from there. Write it in your diary – writing from the left.

Another idea is to write a list of jobs needed per room, and pin that on the back of each door. Then really enjoy ticking off the jobs.

> *I went into our kids' bedrooms, they're teenagers now, and could see clothes, school stuff, plates of old food and stuff everywhere really. No surprises, but I also saw the maintainance jobs piling up - a curtain hanging off, a window that wouldn't shut properly. I made a list of jobs for each room, and over the summer holidays, got most of it done.*
>
> *- Paula, 57*

If you need help to tidy up, read *The Gentle Art of Swedish Death Cleaning*, by Margareta Magnusson, where she encourages the reader in a lovely, no-nonsense Scandinavian way to take responsibility for your stuff and not to leave it all as a burden for family and friends.

Marie Kondo's *The Life-Changing Magic of Tidying* is also a popular book that will help you clear out those drawers in a way that'll make you feel energised. You might think it sounds bonkers – but it works.

Decluttering is particularly end-of-life changing for those who survive you.

Making plans to sort your stuff out

Think about what a great relief it will be to have had a big tidy up. But do you have to do it on your own? Is there someone who could help you? (Other people will find your mess easier to sort out than you will. Perhaps you can pay a young person to help?)

What needs to be done?

Ideally, when do you want to have done this by?

Do you need help? If so, from who?

When will you start? Put it in your diary.

How will it feel to have done this?

So we hope that will help with the physical stuff in your home. The next bit is to think some more about other end-of-life arrangements you need to make to help you, and your loved ones. Discussing your own funeral with your family might sound hard, but see what happened in Nina's family when her mum treated her death and funeral almost as if she was talking about how to tackle clearing out a room.

A good death-planning conversation:

What really pushed it was my mum had had a conversation with a friend of hers, who's a real rational, practical sort of person, who said, 'I've decided what I want when I die. I want it like this not like that, and no fuss' and dictated it to her family in quite a brutal way. My mum thought this was a brilliant thing, and had some tentative conversations with each of us. We were able to give her some feedback, and say to her, 'Mum, there are lots of people who really love you, and having a "no fuss" policy when you're dead, deprives them of any opportunity to say goodbye, to recognise their loss. Maybe it doesn't need to be quite so rigid as that.'

So we started talking about her death, her funeral. She was sort of saying put me in a cardboard box, no ceremony. We were able to soften her on that, and bizarrely it's not all about her wishes.

That prompted us to have a much bigger conversation, not all these separate ones.

A friend of mine's partner died recently, he'd been ill but it was very unexpected. They weren't married, and she has found that enormously difficult, because there was no plan in place with his family for how to manage his death. She has been completely excluded, because it wasn't clear beforehand.

My siblings and I were all in the same room with Mum, so we all heard first-hand what Mum's wishes were, what we all wanted and what our anxieties were.

We booked it in - an appointment - and we stuck to it. Just us kids, without partners. We talked about practicalities, financial planning, mapping out some scenarios, the foundations really. Then Mum was able to talk about what she wanted for end of life, the funeral and after the funeral.

Having the conversations did feel very uncomfortable and all of us were in tears at one point, with different things triggered in different individuals – it's very emotional. Even the thought that at some point Mum won't be here is almost unbearable, but it is clearly going to happen. It was difficult emotionally, but that isn't a reason not to have the conversation, and we now have Mum's wishes and our concerns clear. And I think when that day comes, we have something to refer back to.

We noted physical items – things Mum wanted to give to people – so who should get what is written down. There were several items none of us wanted, and some items we all wanted! Actually, it's not about money, it's about sentimental value – having those conversations when we're all reasonable, because Mum is still alive. I can't imagine having those conversations when you're in the middle of grieving, and all the emotional turmoil, and funerals, probate, house sales, whatever you're trying to do. So you and your siblings being as steady as you can be makes the conversation much easier.'

– Nina, 51

Make a will

Making a will need not be expensive or difficult. Not having a will or estate planning is crazy and costly. It makes no sense – 31 million UK adults think, 'Oh yes, I plan to make a will when I'm older.' You could be dead tomorrow, so do you want to have a say in who gets the special teapot?

Put it in your diary today.

In our experience, it's a huge relief to have it crossed off the list.

> *We live in the country with farming communities all around and I've seen so much suffering when people die without a will - farm bank accounts frozen, livestock going unfed. Make a will. Make a will now!*
> *- Isobel Webster, charity worker*

Your end-of-life wishes

There might come a time you feel you've completed enough of what you came here to do. Perhaps you'll know when that is, but it might slip beyond your control – decisions on your treatment and whether to keep you alive, or not.

Have a conversation with those who matter, and list your end-of-life wishes. You may also want to consult a solicitor or will writer to help with this.

Do you want medical staff and family to go to any lengths and any cost to extend your life?

An advance decision or living will can make it easier for you and kinder for your loved ones – highlighting what's important for you to be comfortable.

If you want to refuse potentially life-sustaining treatment, your decision must be in writing, signed, witnessed, and include the statement 'even if life is at risk as a result'.

In Atul Gawande's book *Being Mortal*, he talks of a man

who communicated clearly that he would be happy just to end his days at home if he can sit in his chair, watch football on TV and eat ice cream. His preferred end-of-life wish.

Lasting power of attorney

This is a legal document that gives someone you nominate the power to act on your behalf in financial or medical decisions if you are incapable of doing so. You can only set up a lasting power of attorney while you still have the ability to make decisions for yourself. This is known as 'mental capacity'. There is plenty of information about this online or from your legal or financial adviser, but the important thing is to do this while you still can.

Action:

Remember to pay attention to your roots as you do this.

What are the steps you need to take to:
- Write a will
- Write an advance decision (living will)
- Organise a lasting power of attorney?

When will you do each step?

Get the conversation started

Studies have shown that while a minority shirked from end-of-life care discussion, most would welcome it but were rarely given the opportunity. From our experience, just getting the conversation started with a loved one is the hardest. In the context of people being terminally ill, a useful sentence can be: 'What do you know about what's happening to you, and how do you feel about that?'

Make your wishes known

Extend life or not? As we are living longer, the arguments for not artificially extending life become better. It's not only about economics, although a huge percentage, around 30%, of medical care budgets are currently spent in the last weeks of life.

Hospital or home. Most people prefer to do their dying at home not in hospital, but without instructions to the contrary, medical professionals will do their best to extend your life – which may be the opposite of what you want.

What makes a good funeral?

> When I was younger I hated going to weddings. It seemed that all of my aunts and the grandmotherly types used to come up to me, poking me in the ribs and cackling, telling me, 'You're next.'
>
> They stopped that shit after I started doing the same thing to them at funerals.
>
> - Anonymous

You've been to lots of funerals . . . think about the good ones, and some you don't want to remember.

A good funeral

> Dad died suddenly, almost ten years after retiring. Frankly, he'd been a clever, cantankerous, funny but often unhappy person and an alcoholic. With the family we were discussing what to do for his funeral and it was a problem until we reminded each other he

liked vanilla ice cream, red tulips, and his favourite music was the Beethoven Emperor Piano Concerto and anything played on a cinema organ. From there we had the basis of the funeral.

The problem of what to say that honoured the truth of his life was solved when his son-in-law, John, coined a recurrent refrain for the eulogy: 'Roderick was an impossible person', which he then spun in various ways – an impossible combination of a Plymouth Brethren builder's son and academic philosopher; a burly, bluff, no-nonsense rugby-loving Kiwi who cried at old war films; an intellectual sophisticate who loved ice cream, tennis and baking bread. The 'impossible person' motif then gave John scope to allude to some of the darker dimensions of Roderick's impossibility. At one point drawing an analogy with a musical instrument – 'fine-tuned and highly strung' – and he said that, sometimes, strings broke . . .

It was lovely to see his old colleagues and those who'd known him well wandering round after the service with a cone of vanilla ice cream. It worked.

— Diana, daughter

Find a good person to take your funeral

Reactions to my 400+ funerals have included: 'That was really lovely.' Or 'I'm not supposed to say that I enjoyed that, but that was great.' I get chocolates, flowers, wine. I get people saying thanks for telling the truth, thanks for making us laugh.

One person said he liked the funeral I took so much, would I take his wedding.

No two deaths are alike. People care – they don't care. There's love – there's no love. There's flowers – no flowers. In the end there's great equality in death, you deserve the best I can give you.

When planning a funeral, I ask what would the deceased have liked. Emotional intelligence is needed – it's about what's authentic and real. Telling the truth in a way that's honest, but palatable.

- Ollie, funeral celebrant

Nothing ceremonial

As to the funeral, my mother-in-law wanted nothing ceremonial, just a little gathering at home where she'd celebrated many happy family events. As it turned out there were over 30 people there, not bad when you consider, at 93, most of her friends were dead.

The guests played a little game, using her much-loved biscuit tin which had always been full of home baking. Each person wrote down what they remembered about her on a slip of paper, popped it in the tin, and at the end, everyone pulled one out and read it aloud. Thus passed a very happy, yet tearful afternoon with many contributing however they wished.

- Liz, early 60s

Funerals good and bad

Make some notes about what for you makes a good and a bad funeral. Ask your friends, make it fun to discuss.

> Out with friends one evening, a warm late summer glow falls on every smiling face. Then it lands on you, out of nowhere. Like a punch. She's not there. She will never be.
> – Martin Wroe, from his poem 'Cherish'

TAKE
CARE

Reality check: Where are you now with death?

Continue to take care of yourself with this. We've thrown a lot of heavy stuff in here — more than any other Act 3 concept so far. You need to evaluate this for yourself, and of course . . . make a plan.

Look at the wheel below, and draw it as big as you can in your journal pages.

Some people say it looks like a pizza. Label your slices: attitude, purpose, values, key relationships, wills and wishes, tidy up and funeral.

1. **Write positively, what you want or need for each category in a sentence:** '*I want to write my will.*'
2. **Scale from 1 to 10 in each section your progress towards that goal:** '*I do think about it a bit, so I'll give it a 3/10.*'
3. **Write what action you will take to move your score up towards your goal:** '*I'll draft thoughts for my will, before making an appointment with a will writer.*'
4. **Beside each action write when you will do this:** '*Saturday afternoon, between 2 and 4. The family are visiting on Sunday, so that will spur me to do it.*'

MY GOOD DEATH WHEEL

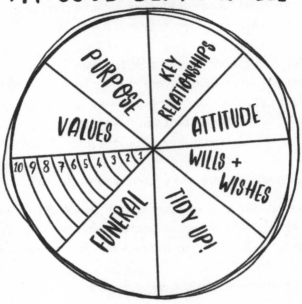

Below is a full example of a completed wheel.

Attitude: *I accept I will die, and I want be proactive about how I approach my own death.*

Currently, I recognise I don't want to face my own death, so I'll score that 3/10.

To change that, I'm going to find out on Friday afternoon about a lasting power of attorney.

Purpose: *I want to feel I gave life in Act 3 my best shot.*

I only have vague ideas of what I want to aim for in Act 3, so I'll score that 4/10. I'll make a list on Sunday afternoon.

Values: *Kindness and consideration have always mattered to me, so I want to leave my affairs in order.*

At the moment, my will is very out of date. I'll score this 5/10, because at least I have a will! I'll book an appointment on Monday with the will writer.

Key relationships: *I want to make sure my family know I love them, and that I haven't left a big mess for them to deal with.*

I think they know I love them, but I hardly ever say it or write it. I'll score this 6/10. I'm going to write to each of them by the end of this month.

Mess: I'm going to put an hour in the diary each Monday to do some computer decluttering, passwords and so on. I'll make some more videos on my phone explaining how to fix some of the stuff in the house I look after. That's about 3/10 – I've made a start, but quite a long way to go.

Wills and Wishes: *My goal is to have all of this done by the end of the month.*

I have thought about it, and I wrote a will many years ago. I need a lasting power of attorney though. I'll score this section 3/10. My first step is to have a conversation after supper tonight with my partner.

Tidy up: *My goal is to have sorted out each part of the house by the end of the year.*

Some attempt has been made, but in reality it's 5/10. I'll start next Saturday by making a list of what's needed in each room.

Funeral: *I have some idea of what a good, and a bad funeral is like.*

I think this will get sorted when I do my advance decision, which I want to do over the next bank holiday weekend. It scores 2/10 for now, as I have never talked about or written down what my own funeral wishes are.

> Death may be the greatest of
> all human blessings.
>
> — Socrates[6]

The death of others

A sad truth of Act 3 and Act 4 is the inevitable increase of our peers dropping off the perch.

> *My handbag is filling up with funeral service sheets*
> *— Dawn, Judy's mum*

Your death is not the only one to manage well. How do we deal with the deaths of others?

What *not* to say when someone is bereaved

People want to be helpful in the face of bereavement, but often say shockingly insensitive things, or point out positives that a bereaved person does not want to hear.

> *'At least she lived a long life.'*
>
> *'At least you have other family.'*
>
> *'Oh, my brother died last year . . .'*
>
> *'You're young enough to find someone else . . .'*

Don't try to cheer them up or give unasked for advice. But neither ignore the person's bereavement; acceptance will come in time, but nobody knows how long that will take. Think ahead – what would be a simple, sensitive response?

What to say when someone is bereaved

I saw a person on the other side of the street, I'd heard his partner had recently died. I hardly knew him, but I crossed the road and just said to him, 'I don't know what to say . . .' We became friends. He is now my partner.
- Anonymous

Empathy: *'I'm so sorry to hear Fred died.'* Note: mention their name and 'died'.

Standing alongside them in their pain and grief – silence, but be present, not checking your phone, or changing the subject.

Acknowledge their loss: *'It must be so hard for you.'*

Take their feelings seriously – '*I can understand how devastated you are.'* (Even if you don't feel it.)

Don't try to fix it or make them feel better: Grief is important and needs time. '*Who knows how long this will take for you to feel OK; I'm still here.'*

Don't avoid them: *'I'm happy to call each Sunday if you would like that.'*

If we're wise, we become barometers for pain - a safe pair of arms to be hugged by. A safe pair of ears to listen. A safe brain to help in thinking what to do next. I'm a Saint Bernard dog, I hold people in the moment wherever they are, because somebody did it for me. I learned to spend myself on others because it's the decent thing to do.

- Ollie, funeral celebrant

Cherish

We choose to remember the one we have lost, to treasure who they were and how they made us.

We choose a kind of acceptance, without knowing we have chosen. Maybe we choose company and conversation. Maybe solitude.

We choose to recognise our mortality, to face our fear kindly. We choose to look at ourselves face to face, to look our own death in the eye.

To bow down low.

Life respecting death.

We choose to give away our time before time gives us away.

To cherish these days we have and those we share them with.

– Martin Wroe, from his poem 'Cherish'[8]

Look after the widows and widowers

An analysis of findings in the English Longitudinal Study of Ageing identified over-50s as a group particularly at risk of loneliness and the likely triggers for that. For example, widowers are more than 5 times as likely to report feeling 'often lonely' as peers who are in a relationship.

What to do for the bereaved

> *When my father died, a kind neighbour placed a lit candle in a jam jar on my doorstep. It was a gentle, sweet reminder of her support.*
>
> *- Jackie*

- Keep giving them hugs
- Offer to go with them to register the death and make funeral plans
- Make meals and run errands – perhaps set up a rota
- Keep inviting them – don't assume they're too sad to go out
- Put dates in your diary, to jog your memory to keep in touch, especially around festive holidays, birthdays and anniversaries
- Drop round – don't feel you have to wait to be invited.
- Make a note to send flowers or a card a few months after the bereavement

Only grieving can heal grief; the passage of time will lessen the acuteness, but time alone without the direct experience of grief, will not heal it.
– Anne Lamott, *Traveling Mercies: Some Thoughts on Faith*[8]

Life after death

In our opinion we are spiritual beings. Religious faith is a personal choice which spawns love, not judgement, of others. We have seen the major religions serve people brilliantly at every stage of life, *and* sometimes they can be a problem.

How you address any faith beliefs about the end of life is entirely up to you.

There certainly is life after death

Amelia Thomas' husband had been hit by a car after which she nursed him through 3 difficult years until he died at age 67.

> *It took me three years to deal with his suffering, but the important thing afterwards was to accept my own suffering. When I did so it was quite cathartic. I wept and wept. Having done so it's been much easier to move forward, which I have. I was then able to make progress. Six years after his death I suddenly realised that all the people who are now dear to me my husband had never known! This was an enormous moment and I realised I had made a new life for myself!*

New love can be found after death

Peggy, widowed at 73 – after 49 years of marriage – became friends with Don, also widowed. Two years later, he asked her to marry him. Eventually she said yes, but warned him, 'I might only survive a few months!' In November 2018, they celebrated their 21st wedding anniversary.

Death Café

Until we attended a local Death Café, it wasn't obvious to us just how many questions there are that anyone can have about death. Death Café is a wonderful worldwide resource. Anyone can meet to talk about any and every aspect of death in small groups over tea and cake. Over 7,000 events have been held in 58 countries. Their goal is *'to increase awareness of death with a view to helping people make the most of their finite lives'*.

At an event we attended someone on our table opened with 'I just don't know what to say to someone who is bereaved ...' which triggered a long and profound conversation that could have gone on for hours.

If the Death Café idea is intriguing to you, we want to encourage you to give it a go, or possibly set one up – visit www.deathcafe.com.

And finally...

Several people told us what their priorities would be if – in reasonable health – they found they had a month to live:

> *First and foremost, well before tidying up ... with a month to live I'd enjoy writing letters to family and friends who have been important to me in my life and telling them things I may not have felt able to say when I might have done, for a variety of reasons. I might enclose a memento with the letter. It would be a loving and cathartic experience.*
>
> *- Vera*

> *I'd see everyone I care about. Have some treats. Not be a drama queen.*
>
> *- Andrew*

I'd do some of the things I have been too afraid or reticent to do up to now. Not skydiving or snowboarding, more snoozing and snogging!

- Kitty

Family. Close friends. Champagne.

- Robert

I'd try to get my husband to take time off . . . might take a trip to the sea.

- Dorothy

Waste some pension funds!

- Julia

I'd live the last month as normal. I generally make my peace with people as I go along. We're all human and inevitably disagree with people as we go through life. Make peace when you need to, don't wait for something to happen. Don't have a bucket list - do it now, be spontaneous and live each day as your last. One day you will be right, so don't live with regrets.

- Happiness

What would your priorities be?

One-minute summary: Death

Talking about death won't kill you. Mulling its existence and making plans around death with others will help you be more in control around your mortality — which of course is the ultimate loss of control. Death planning is an act of kindness for yourself and those you love. Regularly remembering you are mortal can increase your appreciation of and zest for life. Act now.

Obviously, moving from Act 3 to Act 4 means increased health issues, the loss of people we love and more funerals to attend. Though a very painful time of life, those who learn what to say and do alongside people suffering or bereaved find it a great relief. And they're good to have around.

Losing loved ones doesn't have to mean your life is over too, although no one can say how long it might take you to adapt to your loss. We have been inspired by those who have found ways to help their recovery, and even blossomed following major bereavements.

Chapter Ten

The End – Or Is It the Beginning?

You cannot go back and change the
beginning, but you can start where you
are and change the ending.

– James R. Sherman, *Rejection*[1]

Start where you are

We started and finish this book with these same words, and what's most powerful in the saying above is the word 'can'.

you *can* start where you are and
change the ending

It's not always easy – we carry many bags, boxes and baggage by this time in our lives. It's easier to focus on the negative parts of our life story so far, but we hope this book has spurred you on to focus on the gratitude for what you have had, and still have.

And could have.

Finally, you're still here on earth, so why not try to enjoy it; and I mean all those simple things that everyone has – cosiness in winter, the wonders of spring, the moon, the stars, a cup or glass of what you fancy, watching birds, people – stay interested in this fantastic EARTH.

– Dame Eileen Atkins

A better Act 3 comes from laying your burden down, one bag, box or basket at a time. Keep using your journal to do that, and create more journals when this one is full.

You'll feel lighter.

You can do more.

Having put down a burden you might want to put more and more baggage down.

It will make space for the new.

Act 3 - Actions and outcomes

Last February, I decided that plans for the next chapter in my life needed some serious consideration. I stumbled upon an advertisement for an 'Act 3' workshop and it seemed a good place to start.

All I knew was that the challenges I faced were probably familiar to many others in my age group. Ageing parents, ageing partner; and although my career had sustained me both creatively and financially for the better part of 30 years, it still felt as though there were many new paths to travel (and I was really looking for a change).

To be honest it all felt daunting and I'd reached a crossroad. I'd put a lot on hold. So the workshop definitely kick-started a process. It gave me an opportunity to look at the issues in an informal way; this was both good and challenging. Once I'd identified and acknowledged some of the fears (and ways in which I limited myself. . .), it became easier to recognise old patterns and to see what was holding me back.

In making some lists and mind-mapping, I was able to identify what really excited me and what I could plan for. Once I had a plan to try and do an MA, the next steps were more straightforward. Practical applications, looking at finances and visiting colleges.

There were doubts along the way. . . but somehow these diminished as I became more able to access my own convictions. I'm now on a full-time course in London. It's fantastic to be a student again, and although there's still a lot of juggling (and doubting!), the journey so far has been exhilarating.

Thanks to Act 3 . . .

– Georgina Hall

If you remember one thing from this book – let it be this:

Get back to what's important for you – your roots.

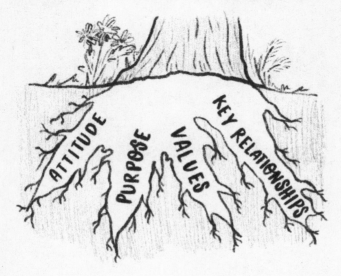

Life will follow.

We want to thank you for investing your time and energy in reading this book, and we hope it is already bearing fruit for you. Our wish is that this book will be useful, loved and shared. That has been our goal in writing it.

Please let us know — we would love to hear what is making your Act 3 work best for you.

Judy and Adrian Reith   www.act3life.com

Resources

We've tried to be as helpful as we can below with resources, but please check our website www.act3life.com for more up-to-date help with Act 3.

TAKE CARE

Throughout the book we've put the Take Care symbol. Just to remind you, it means to take care of yourself, which is sometimes harder than it sounds. In which case there's plenty of good professional help available. Sometimes you'll find the first doctor or therapist you might talk to may not be right for you – if so, ask to speak to another one.

TAKE CARE

We recommend you find counselling or psychotherapy through one of the professional organisations.

British Association of Counselling and Psychotherapy
www.bacp.co.uk

Association of Family Therapy
www.aft.org.uk

Relate
www.relate.org.uk

The Tavistock Centre for Couples Relationships offers online counselling as well as in person, and a brief course for anyone over 50.

Couples MOT
www.tavistockrelationships.org

Dating for over 50s
www.lumenapp.com

LGBTQ help
www.switchboard.lgbt

Frazzled Café
Regular meet-ups in Marks and Spencer's cafés to talk and listen in a safe place when life all gets too much and stress takes over. Founded by Ruby Wax.
www.frazzledcafe.org

Laughter Therapy
www.laughtertherapy.org.uk

BOOKS and LINKS

We have bought more books than we can ever read. And especially about ageing and Act 3. Then there's all the websites, podcasts and other resources. Below we have listed some of the books we have found helpful under six categories: Roots, Health and Fitness, the Branches of the Tree, Transition, Dying and General Act 3 reading.

Roots

Anam Cara: Spiritual Wisdom from the Celtic World, by John O'Donohue (Transworld Ireland, 1999)

Falling Upward: A Spirituality for the Two Halves of Life, by Richard Rohr (SPCK, 2012)

Finding Meaning in the Second Half of Life: How to Finally, Really Grow Up, by James Hollis (Avery, 2006)

LifeLines: Notes on Life & Love, Faith & Doubt, by Malcolm

Doney and Martin Wroe (Unbound, 2018)

Not That Kind of Love: A Sister, A Brother, Some Tumours and a Cat, by Clare and Greg Wise (Quercus, 2018)

The Road Back to You: An Enneagram Journey to Self-Discovery, by Ian Morgan Cron and Suzanne Stabile (IVP Books, 2016)

The Second Curve: Thoughts on Reinventing Society, by Charles Handy (Random House, 2016)

Volunteering
www.volunteeringmatters.org.uk

School Readers
www.schoolreaders.org

Gransnet
www.gransnet.com

Health and Fitness

Just Move! A New Approach to Fitness After 50, by James P. Owen (National Geographic, 2016)

Run for Your Life: How One Woman Ran Circles Around Breast Cancer, by Jenny Baker (Pitch Publishing, 2017)

Here are the links to more academic research on the reality of wearable technology:

The dark side of wearable fitness trackers
www.iflscience.com/technology/how-we-discovered-dark-side-wearable-fitness-trackers

Changing algorithms in wearable trackers changes outcomes
https://blogs.bmj.com/bjsm/2017/01/20/not-steps-equalchanging-algorithms-wearable-trackers-changes-outcomes

Slimming World
www.slimmingworld.co.uk

Branches of the Tree

How Many Friends Does One Person Need? Dunbar's Number and Other Evolutionary Quirks, by Robin Dunbar (Faber and Faber, 2011)

How to Find Fulfilling Work, by Roman Krznaric, The School of Life (Macmillan, 2012)

Not Fade Away: How to Thrive in Retirement, by Celia Dodd (Bloomsbury Publishing, 2018)

Play: How it Shapes the Brain, Opens the Imagination, and Invigorates the Soul, by Stuart Brown (Avery, 2010)

Michael Leunig, Australian cartoonist, poet and cultural commentator
www.leunig.com.au

Local Treasures – a recruitment agency with an emphasis on offering employment where experience and wisdom, particularly found in the over 50s, is valued!
www.localtreasures.me

Support and information for career change, jobs and volunteering for the over 50s
www.restless.co.uk

Co-housing
www.cohousing.org.uk

For those without children – resources, training and support
www.awwoc.org

For financial advice, check the Financial Conduct Authority website to find reliable providers
www.fca.org.uk

National Council for Voluntary Organisations – database and information on local and national volunteering organisations and opportunities
www.ncvo.org.uk

Action Button – use your voice and take action on the news that matters
www.actionbutton.org

The Enneagram: There are many personality-type indicators. For most of our shared life, we have found The Enneagram especially helpful in understanding each other. If you want to know more: www.enneagraminstitute.com

Transition
Transitions: Making Sense of Life's Changes, by William Bridges, revised 25th anniversary edtion (Da Capo Press, 2004)

Dying
Feel the Fear and Do It Anyway, by Susan Jeffers (Vermillion, 2007)
The Top Five Regrets of the Dying, by Bronnie Ware (Hay House, 2012)

I'm Dead, Now What? Important Information About My Belongings, Business Affairs, and Wishes (Peter Pauper Press, 2014). A write-in journal with well-structured questions to help you record the important stuff

Death Café – meetings in cafes to talk about all aspects of
death and dying
www.deathcafe.com

National Will Writers Association
www.nationalwillwriters.co.uk

Bereavement
www.cruse.org.uk
www.griefworks

Celebrants – resources are listed here:
www.goodfuneralguide.co.uk

General Act 3

Bolder: Making the Most of our Longer Lives, by Carl Honoré
(Simon & Schuster, 2018)
Call the Midlife, by Chris Evans (Orion Books, 2015)
*Happy Retirement: The Psychology of Reinvention, A Practical Guide
to Planning and Enjoying the Retirement You've Earned,* by
Kenneth S. Shultz (Dorling Kindersley, 2015)
*Living the Life More Fabulous: Beauty, Style and Empowerment for
Older Women,* by Tricia Cusden (Orion Books, 2018)
Time for Lights Out, by Raymond Briggs (Jonathan Cape, 2019)
The 100-Year Life: Living and Working in an Age of Longevity, by
Lynda Gratton and Andrew Scott (Bloomsbury, 2017)

The Silver Line – helpline, support and information for older
people
www.silverline.org.uk

Need cheering up?

Download Jenni Eclair and Judith Holder's podcast: 'Older and Wider'

Age UK
www.ageuk.org.uk

Alzheimer's
www.alzheimers.org.uk

Caring for Elders – offers workshops and support for anyone who supports an older person
www.caring4elders.co.uk

University of the Third Age
www.u3a.org.uk

The Third Act – offers coaching, workshops and resources for those in Act 3
www.thethirdact.ie

Judy and Adrian Reith's latest information on workshops and coaching
www.act3life.com

Notes

Chapter one

1. James R. Sherman, *Rejection*, Pathway Books, Golden Valley, Minnesota, 1982, p. 45. (This quote is often wrongly attributed to C.S. Lewis.)
2. Frequently attributed to Picasso, however, there's no record of him saying it.
3. A saying often attributed to Einstein, without evidence.
4. John O'Donohue, *Eternal Echoes*, HarperCollins, London, 2000, p. 11.

Chapter two

1. Susie Steiner, 'Top Five Regrets of the Dying', 1 Feb 2012. Used with kind permission. Extracted from the *Guardian*, www.theguardian.com/lifeandstyle/2012/feb/01/top-five-regrets-of-the-dying [08.10.2019]

Chapter three

1. Michelle Obama, Remarks by the First Lady at Tuskegee University Commencement Address, Tuskegee, Alabama, 9 May 2015. https://obamawhitehouse.archives.gov/the-press-office/2015/05/09/remarks-first-lady-tuskegee-university-commencement-address. [08.10.2019]
2. Adam Phillips, used with kind permission of the author.
3. Henry Ford was possibly quoting *'Possunt quia posse videntur.'* 'They can, because they think they can.' Virgil, *The Aeneis of Virgil*,

translated into blank verse by Joseph Trapp, Professor of Poetry in the University of Oxford, remarks upon the fifth book, quote p. 427, published in London, 1718.

4. Viktor Frankl, *Man's Search for Meaning*, Rider, London, 2011.

5. Atul Gawande, *Being Mortal*, Profile Books, London, 2015. Used with kind permission.

6. Irvine Welsh, *Trainspotting*, Vintage, London, 1994. Used with kind permission of the publisher.

7. Jim Carrey, Golden Globe Awards speech, 2016. https://youtu.be/ YHIZ0Rb7lv0 [09.10.2019]

8. Brené Brown, *The Power of Vulnerability*, TED Talk https://www.ted. com/talks/brene_brown_on_vulnerability [09.10.2019]

9. T.S. Eliot, 'The Dry Salvages', from *Four Quartets*, T.S. Eliot, Faber and Faber Ltd, London, 1998. Used with kind permission.

10. Martin Luther King, Jr., *Rediscovering Lost Values,* Sermon at Detroit's Second Baptist Church, 28 February 1954.

11. Bill Bernbach, legendary advertising pioneer. https://www. huffpost.com/entry/advertising-agencies-intellectual-proper- ty_b_994091?guce_referrer=aHR0cHM6Ly93d3cuZ29vZ2x- lLmNvbS8&guce_referrer_sig=AQAAAJ6JybvneAUXwr4C- JIYOpAEhcwcXvdzuzA0IrdopDoBYxrcwdO--QIwbqb-I9X- VCxpRJNmPjffOQnMFASsS6zOqORKzwAMw8sl6j1mvykO- hLQJ2fWyDpj9tNjSNNxit5mLR0z0ICe1dvnmvgd75Yf5ai5_ jba-PGxPc0sW9EzvSY&guccounter=2 [09.10.19]

12. An old joke first recorded in a New Zealand Tablet 18·Oct 1873. *'Them's my principles; but if you don't like them — I kin change them!*

13. Ubuntu philosophy. https://en.wikipedia.org/wiki/Ubuntu_ philosophy [09.10.19]

14. Naomi Gryn, used with kind permission.

15. 'Forgiveness: Letting go of grudges and bitterness', summary of Mayo Clinic article 4 Nov 2017. https://www.mayoclinic.org/ healthy-lifestyle/adult-health/in-depth/forgiveness/art-20047692 [09.10.19]

16. Steve Turner. Used with kind permission of the author.
17. *The Bible*, I Corinthinans 13:4–8, English Standard Version.

Chapter four

1. Thomas Fuller, *Gnomologia: Adegies and Proverbs; Wise Sentences and Witty Sayings,* collected by Thomas Fuller, 1732. Saying number 2479.

2. World Health Organization constitution, 1948. www.who.int/about/who-we-are/constitution [02.10.2019]

3. Edward Smith-Stanley, three times UK Prime Minister. https://medium.com/@steveagyeibeyondlifestyle/those-who-think-they-have-no-time-for-healthy-eating-will-sooner-or-later-have-to-find-time-for-c745d957374a [09.10.19]

4. 'Brisk walking and physical inactivity in 40 to 60 year olds', Public Health England. https://www.gov.uk/government/publications/brisk-walking-and-physical-inactivity-in-40-to-60-year-olds/brisk-walking-and-physical-inactivity-in-40-to-60-year-olds [09.10.2019]

5. James P. Owen, author of *Just Move! A New Approach to Fitness After 50.* https://www.youtube.com/watch?v=J8KYa0afo5o. [09.10.2019]

6. John Geddes. Used with kind permission. https://www.theguardian.com/science/2018/feb/21/the-drugs-do-work-antidepressants-are-effective-study-shows. [09.10.2019]

Chapter five

1. Attributed to W. H. Auden, source unknown.

2. Karl Thompson, 'What Percentage of Your Life Will You Spend at Work?', 16 Aug 2016. https://revisesociology.com/2016/08/16/percentage-life-work. [09.10.2019]

3. Paul Schrader. Used with kind permission Schrader Productions, 03.04.2019

4. Steve Jobs, Stanford Commencement address, 12 June 2005. https://news.stanford.edu/news/2005/june15/jobs-061505.html [09.10.2019] Used with kind permission.

5. Thomas Merton. www.goodreads.com/quotes/88921-discovering-vocation-does-not-mean-scrambling-toward-some-prize-just. [09.10.2019]

6. Frederick Beuchner. https://www.goodreads.com/quotes/158523-listen-to-your-life-see-it-for-the-fathomless-mystery [09.10.2019]

7. Atributed to Sigmund Freud, source unknown.

8. A variant of Karl Groos, *Die Spiele der Thiere* (*The Play of Animals*), 1896, p. 68: '*The animals do not play because they are young, but they have a youth because they must play.*'

9. Robert Waldinger, *What Makes A Good Life? Lessons from the longest study on happiness.* TEDxBeaconStreet, https://www.ted.com/talks/robert_waldinger_what_makes_a_good_life_lessons_from_the_longest_study_on_happiness? [09.10.2019]

10. Attributed to Mark Twain.

11. Dr Stuart Brown, *Play: how it shapes the brain, opens the imagination, and invigorates the soul,* Avery, US edition, 2009.

12. Chuck Palahniuk, *Fight Club,* W. W. Norton & Company, New York, 1996, p. 44. Used with kind permission.

13. Angela Neustatter, *A Home for the Heart,* Gibson Square Books, London, 2014.

14. Maya Angelou, *All God's Children Need Travelling Shoes,* Virago, London, 1987.

15. John Mbiti, African theologian and philosopher. https://en.wikipedia.org/wiki/Ubuntu_philosophy. [09.10.2019]

16. A.A. Milne, extract from *The House at Pooh Corner.* © The Trustees of the Pooh Properties 1928. Published by Egmont UK Ltd and used with permission.

17. Julianne Holt-Lundstad, Timothy B. Smith, J. Bradley Layton, *Social Relationships and Mortality Risk: A Meta-analytic Review.* https://journals.plos.org/plosmedicine/article?id=10.1371/journal.pmed.1000316. [09.10.2019]

18. Pádraig Ó Tuama, TEDx Talk. https://www.youtube.com/watch?v=IJfBYz6tab8

19. Charles Handy, source unknown.

20. Charles Dickens, *David Copperfield,* 1849, page 214, First Avenue Editions.

21. William Bruce Cameron, *Informal Sociology: A Casual Introduction to Sociological Thinking,* Random House, New York, 1963.

22. Barry Schwartz, *The Paradox of Choice,* TEDTalk, 2005. https://www.youtube.com/watch?v=VO6XEQIsCoM [09.10.2019]

23. Arleen Lorrance was possibly inspired by this quote by Gandhi: 'We but mirror the world. All the tendencies present in the outer world are to be found in the world of our body. If we could change ourselves, the tendencies in the world would also change. As a man changes his own nature, so does the attitude of the world change towards him. This is the divine mystery supreme. A wonderful thing it is and the source of our happiness. We need not wait to see what others do.' From Vol 13: 153, *General Knowledge About Health,* p. 241, printed in the *Indian Opinion* on 9 August 1913 from *The Collected Works of M. K. Gandhi,* published by The Publications Division, New Delhi, India, 1958.

24. Paraphrase of a story by Loren Eiseley, 'The Star Thrower' is part of an essay of the same name in *The Unexpected Universe,* Harcourt, Brace & World, 1969. https://en.wikipedia.org/wiki/The_Star_Thrower [09.10.2019]

25. Naomi Gryn, used with kind permission.

26. Sarah Dunant, used with kind permission.

27. Harry Leslie Smith, author of *Don't Let My Past Be Your Future,* source unknown.

28. President Barack Obama, Whitehouse Global Development Summit, 2016. https://obamawhitehouse.archives.gov/the-press-office/2016/07/20/remarks-president-white-house-summit-global-development [17.10.2019]

29. Denis Healey, 1917–2015. 'Ed lacks charisma, and the coalition is doomed - just two of the diktats of Denis Healey, Labour's elder statesman', *Evening Standard* paraphrase, 28 Sept 2011. https://

www.standard.co.uk/news/ed-lacks-charisma-and-the-coalition-is-doomed-just-two-of-the-diktats-of-denis-healey-labours-elder-6447911.html [17.10.2019]

30. Winston Churchill, *Unemployment*, speech at Kinnaird Hall, Dundee, Scotland, 10 October 1908, in *Liberalism and the Social Problem*, 1909, Churchill, Echo Library, 2007, p. 87.

31. Rob Siltanen, TV commercial script for Apple, TBWA/Chiat/Day, aired on TV 1997.

32. Margaret Mead, American cultural anthropologist. Source unknown.

33. Dr Carl Jung, 'Letter to Ms Fanny Bowditch', 22 October 1916, *Letters* Vol. I, p. 33 Princeton University Press, 1973.

34. Michael Leunig. Used with kind permission. Leunig.com.au

Chapter six

1. Lynda Gratton and Andrew Scott, *The 100-Year Life*, Bloomsbury Publishing Plc, © Lynda Gratton and Andrew Scott, 2016, p. 67.

2. Howard Thurman, source unknown.

Chapter seven

1. James Hollis, *Finding Meaning in the Second Half of Life*, Avery, 2006, page 98.

2. Pádraig Ó Tuama, poet, theologian and mediator. www.padraigotuama.com From a quote in a workshop we attended in Febuary 2017. Used with kind permission.

3. John O'Donohue talk at Greenbelt Festival August 2007. https://www.youtube.com/watch?v=iDSw5Vza6Yk [17.10.2019]

4. Herbert 'Harry' Stack Sullivan, American Neo-Freudian psychiatrist and psychoanalyst, 1892–1949. https://www.goodreads.com/author/quotes/225109.Harry_Stack_Sullivan [17.10.2019]

5. A.C. Grayling, British philosopher and author. *The Meaning of Things: Applying Philosophy to life*, Orion; Reprint edition, 9 Aug 2001.

6. Julia Samuel, psychotherapist, interviewed by Joanna Moorhead, 'How to Live and Learn from Loss', *Guardian*, 4 Mar 2017. https://www.theguardian.com/lifeandstyle/2017/mar/04/how-to-live-and-learn-from-great-loss-death [17.10.2019]

7. Loss aversion was first identified by Amos Tversky and Daniel Kahneman. https://en.wikipedia.org/wiki/Loss_aversion

8. Wendy Mitchell. Used with kind permission.

9. Rhian Roberts. Used with kind permission.

Chapter eight

1. William Bridges, *Managing Transitions*, Da Capo Press, 2004. Used with kind permission.

2. Marc Lewis, neuroscientist. Used with kind permission.

3. Muhammad Ali, 1942–2016. *The News* (*The Port Arthur News*), 'Ali wants both Joe, Foreman at same time' (UPI news service), 30 Nov 1974, p. 11, column 3, Port Arthur, Texas.

4. André Gide, *Les faux-monnayeurs* [The Counterfeiters] Nouvell Revue Française, 1925. *On ne découvre pas de terre nouvelle sans consentir à perdre de vue, d'abord et longtemps, tout rivage.*

5. Celia Dodd, *Not Fade Away: How to Thrive in Retirement*, Green Tree, an imprint of Bloomsbury Publishing Plc. © Celia Dodd. Used with kind permission.

Chapter nine

1. Peter Saul, *Let's Talk About Dying*, TEDTalk, 15 July 2015. https://www.ted.com/talks/peter_saul_let_s_talk_about_dying [17.10.2019]

2. Jeffrey Kluger, 'Why Are Old People Less Scared of Dying?', *TIME*, 11 Feb 2016, para. 3. https://time.com/4217039/why-are-old-people-less-scared-of-dying [17.10.2019]

3. Homer Simpson in 'Team Homer', *The Simpsons*, Season 7, Episode 12, 7 Jan 1996. Written by Mike Scully, directed by Mark Kirkland.

4. 'You, Me and the Big C', BBC podcast, 17 Aug 2018. https://www.bbc.co.uk/programmes/p06hqtqc [17.10.2019]
5. Malcom Doney and Martin Wroe, *LifeLines*, Unbound, London, 2018, ch 7.
6. Socrates, Greek philosopher, died 339BC. https://www.goodreads.com/quotes/13057-death-may-be-the-greatest-of-all-human-blessings [17.10.2019]
7. Dawn Orr, Judy's mum, in her twilight years, 2007.
8. Martin Wroe, writer, priest and poet. Used with kind permission.

Chapter ten

1. Anne Lamott, *Traveling Mercies: Some Thoughts on Faith*, Anchor, 2000, p. 63.
2. James R. Sherman, *Rejection*, Pathway Books, 1982, p. 45.

Credit and thanks to these sheroes and heroes

Huge, hearty and healthy thanks to Richard Vincent for his stonking contribution of the health chapter – we've never met anyone so encouraging and full of life. We're also mightily indebted to Malcom Doney and Martin Wroe for forty years of Act 1, 2 and 3 wisdom, inspiration and prodding. Roll on Act 4.

We're grateful on a daily basis to Rosie, Tilly, Phoebe and Nick for what they give us. Thanks also to Douglas Alexander and Jacqui Christian for oomph; Dave and Ange Andrews for a lifetime's love; Dame Eileen Atkins for perspective; Jonny and Jenny Baker for the miles; Roger Bamber and Nicky Napier for cutting through the crap; Nina Barnsely for planning; Nick Battle for gazelles; Michael and Debbie Beckett for shared honesty; Vera Beesley Schuster pour amour; John Best for sonhood; Juliet Bickerton for her delivery; Peter and Caroline Bone for listening; Kirsty Buck and the *Guardian* for Masterclasses; Justin and Nancy Butcher for a step at a time; Liz Curran for a good account; Tricia Cusden for pro-ageing; David and Mary Davies forever; Meryl Doney for warmth; Suzanne and Geoff Doyle Morris for enthusiam; Sarah Dunant for Botcare; Martin and Julia Evans for the fight; Archie Ferguson for tears; The Greenbelt Festival for glue; Kip and Jane Gresham for constancy; Naomi Gryn for motherhood; Simon Gunn for saying no; Georgina Hall for tenacity;

Stu Hallam for straight shooting; Charles and Elizabeth Handy for breakfast; Andy and Sibylle Harrison for fun; Tim and Jane Hawkes for Shiraz and chats; The Hewson Family for the craic; John Hodges for allowing us to pick his brains; Thomas Hillas for elucidation; Emma and Mike Hodgeson for excitement; Martin and Deborah Hofman for climbing mountains; Ruth Holt for threads; Robert Iles for a view; Andrew Ingram for no nonsense; Phil and Steph Johnstone for adventure; Graham Judd for wondering; Craig and Jen Keeler-Milne for the years; Mark Kenner for the long view; Neil Kirby for one liners; Dan Kunkle for thoughts; John Lambie for tenderness; Janey Lee Grace for the Sober Club; Michael Leunig for prophesy; Richard Marks for secrets; Ashley Moffett and Mike Bate for wise chat; Hannah and Jonathan Mayo for fidelity; Simon and Hilary Mayo for white burgundy wisdom; Ian and Susan Mactavish for lunch and laughs; Kate and Rob McCorquodale for encouragement; Diana Mills for revelation; Wendy Mitchell for melting our hearts; Larry Mullen and Anne Acheson for heart and soul; Karen and Harry Napier for sparkle; Patrick O'Gorman for clarity; Ollie and Ted – top dogs; Pádraig Ó Tuama for interpretation; Dorothy and Simon Peyton Jones for astonishment; Angie (Angelica) Phillips for positivity; Mike and Vikki Poole for guts; Arthur Pooley for time; Adrian Rees for light and shade; Angela Reith for harmony; Helen Robbins and Alasdair Cant for mischief; Rhian Roberts for hitting the right note; Chris and Sarah Rose for heart; Cecil Rowe for bravery; Bev Sage and Errol Kennedy for banging the drum; Liz and Steve Scott for a good feed; Kitty Taylor for animation; Steve Turner for a way with words; Meriel Vincent for capers; Isobel Webster for delight; Enid and Willie Williams and David Keleel for illumination; Pip Wilson for Stinking Late; Ed and Brita Wolf for history; Jo and John Wroe for words; Meg Wroe best woman; Julie Wych for snapshots.

The Unbound Team

Dan Kieran for answering our original email; Rachael Kerr for dynamite editing and cheerleading; Imogen Denny and team for dotting 'T's and crossing 'I's and tolerance.

When you get to our age, you struggle to remember your own name, let alone anyone else's. We have a horrible feeling we have forgotten someone who should be thanked. We are very sorry. Get in touch; we owe you lunch.

More about the authors

We help people move on - in a good way

Judy Reith and Adrian Reith are professional coaches and writers. We've been married for 30 years and we have 3 adult children. We are definitely in Act 3.

We work year-round with individuals and groups to create lasting, profound change at all stages of life and particularly in Act 3, using the methods explained in this book. Together we've run multiple *Guardian* Masterclasses, corporate and community seminars and weekend workshops. Get in touch to talk about your Act 3 needs.

Judy Reith, 50-something

Judy had imagined she'd be a perfect mother — until she became a mother. Parenting is the hardest job in the world she discovered, so she got some coaching and started to change her behaviour.

Since then, and having trained as a coach and in parenting education, Judy has helped thousands of parents to have a better relationship with their children through her one-to-one coaching, writing, courses and speaking. She is a regular contributor on TV and radio and 'Pause for Thought' on BBC Radio 2. She is the author of 7 *Secrets of Raising Girls Every Parent Must Know, Be A Great Mum* and the parenting manual *Transform Living with Teenagers*. She is the far-from-perfect mother of 3, now adapting to living in an empty nest with a puppy.

Adrian Reith, 60-something

Adrian spent his first career in business and media as a writer and director in advertising, where he won a number of creative awards. Since retraining, aged 50, he has specialised in facilitation, the coaching of leaders of creative businesses and chaired an international charity, Street Child United. He recently built his own eco house and cycled from Land's End to John o'Groats – all the while watching his 3 daughters with amazement. He has a short attention spa . . .

Index

Act 3, 1–4

adoption, 59–62

advertising and advertisements, 42–3, 143, 191

ageing, and illness, 91

alcohol, 99–100, 112

Alexander, David, 187

Ali, Muhammad, 230

Alzheimer's, 41, 76, 98, 151–2, 217, 223, 225, 245, 277

Andrews, Dave, 161–2, 234

Angelou, Maya, 158

anger, 33, 45, 85, 105, 108, 194, 234

anti-ageing products, 222, 233

anxiety, 77, 104, 108, 110, 112, 169, 179, 182, 234

art therapy, 138

artificial intelligence (AI), 183

Ashe, Arthur, 211

Atkins, Dame Eileen, 188, 267

attitude, 29–30, 31–9

    and beliefs, 34–6

    and labels, 37–8

Auden, W. H., 117

balance, 94–6

Bamber, Roger, 34, 242

Beethoven, Ludwig van, 253

bereavement, 200–1, 258–63, 265, 276

Bernbach, Bill, 55

Beuchner, Frederick, 129

Biddulph, Steve, 244

Bier, Philip, 118

Blake, Eubie, 23

blood pressure, 102

body language, 83

boomerang kids, 76

Boyle, Peter, 120

brain, 103–4

Brexit, 179, 184

Bridges, William, 210, 227–8, 230

Bright, John, 77

Brown, Brené, 48

Brown, Dr Stuart, 134, 136, 145

Browning Wroe, Jo, 150, 152, 156

Bruegel, Pieter, the Elder, 141

Bullmore, Adam, 175

caffeine, 112

Cameron, William Bruce, 173

cancer, 91–2, 98, 108–10, 200, 241–2

care-homes, and children, 136–7
caring, 119
Carrey, Jim, 47–8
Casals, Pablo, 141
charity shops, 160, 188, 217, 224
children's games, 141
Christmas, 161–2
Churchill, Winston, 190
coeliac disease, 186
co-housing movement, 153
commandos, 56–7
concentration camps, 40
Connors, Jimmy, 211
Corinthians, 88
Corymeela Community, 168
Cusden, Tricia, 17, 132
cycling, 5, 93, 188, 210

dancing, 94, 140–1, 213
De Niro, Robert, 120
death, 237–65
 death wheel, 256
 and decluttering, 246–7
 life after death, 261–2
 see also bereavement;
 funerals
Death Café, 262–3, 276
debt, 172–3
decluttering, 246–7
dementia, 92, 108, 110, 165,
 223–6, 238
 see also Alzheimer's
demonstrations, 187

depression, 45, 77, 92, 98, 104,
 108, 110, 112, 230, 234
 play and, 138–9
diabetes, 92
Dickens, Charles, 171
diet, 98–101, 112
dietary supplements, 100
DNA, 91
Dodd, Celia, 235
dog owners, 70
dog-walking, 162, 166, 242
Doney, Malcolm, 245
downsizing, 19, 21, 149, 172
drama therapy, 138
Dunant, Sarah, 183

Einstein, Albert, 139, 279
Eiseley, Loren, 180
Eliot, T. S., 53
Emerson, Ralph Waldo, 159–60
empty nests, 59, 65, 74–5, 153,
 291
end-of-life wishes, 250–2, 257
English Channel, 51
English Longitudinal Study of
 Ageing, 260
Enneagrams, 52, 275
environmental issues, 180–1,
 184
euthanasia, 237
exercise, 91–8
 aerobic, 92–3
 anaerobic, 93

high intensity exercise (HIT), 94
positive feedback, 96–8
and sleep, 113
and stress, 107
eye contact, 83
eyesight, fading, 212, 216, 221

Farah, Mo, 221
fear, 207–11
Financial Conduct Authority, 205
fish, 99
fishing, 143
Ford, Henry, 32
forgiveness, 73, 77, 103, 108–9, 244–5
Frankl, Viktor, 40
Freud, Sigmund, 133
friends, 68–9, 159–68, 244
    see also neighbours
frontal cortex, 137
fruit and vegetables, 99
funerals, 129, 245, 247–9, 252–5, 257, 261

Gandhi, Mahatma, 36, 179, 187
gastric function, 102
Gawande, Atul, 42, 250
Geddes, professor John, 104
generosity, 33, 63, 103, 108, 200
Gide, André, 231
global warming, see environmental issues

goals, 15–20, 133, 144, 157, 167, 178, 191, 196
G.O.A.T.S., 18–21, 133, 144, 157, 167, 178, 191, 196
Gold, Ollie, 129, 254, 260
Gratton, Lynda, 136, 199
Grayling, A. C., 211
grief, 216–17
    see also bereavement
Gryn, Naomi, 75, 181
Guardian Soulmates, 200
gym memberships, 96

Hall, Georgina, 269
Hamilton, Tricia, 128
Handy, Charles, 170
Hannah, John, 126
Harrison, Andrew, 130
Healey, Denis and Edna, 38
healthcare, 186
hearing loss, 213
heart, health and disease, 77, 91–3, 99, 108–9
heart monitors, 96
Henline, Bobby, 221
Hodges, Professor John, 121
Hollis, James, 121, 207–8
Holt, Ruth, 49, 122
home, 146–58
    moving, 155–7
    see also downsizing; empty nests
honesty, 32, 55, 82

hopelessness, 103, 109, 180, 237
hormones, 102
humour, 73, 82, 221, 243

Ikigai, 48–9
immune system, 77, 91–2, 102, 108, 110
inequality, 107
inflammation, 102
inheritance, 175–6
intimacy, 81
Iraq war, 221

James, Oliver, 223
jam-jar bank, 174
Jeffers, Susan, 209
Jerusalem, 46
Jobs, Steve, 121
Johnstone, Phil, 124
Jung, Carl, 193
juvenescence, 136–7

Kahneman, Daniel, 212
Kim Jong-un, 179
kindness, 33, 63, 73, 81
    and death, 242, 256, 264
King, Martin Luther, Jr., 54
Kluger, Jeffrey, 240
Kondo, Marie, 247
Lambie, John, 200–1
Lamott, Anne, 261
lasting power of attorney, 2
    51

leukaemia, 34
Leunig, Michael, 197
Lewis, Marc, 228
lifelong learning, 186
listening, 82–6, 165
Little Red Riding Hood, 238
loneliness, 30, 42, 64, 66–7, 72, 103, 107, 153, 157, 159, 163–4, 188, 190, 237
    bereavement and, 260–1
Lorrance, Arleen, 179
loss, 211–26
    dealing with, 220–1
    and the unexpected, 217–19
loss aversion, 212

Magnusson, Margareta, 246
map reading, 6
Marsh, Sarah, 76
Marx, Groucho, 63
Mbiti, John, 159
Mead, Margaret, 192
memory, 94, 103, 136, 161
memory loss, 223
    see also dementia
menopause, 4, 32, 111–12, 213–14, 227
mental health, 104–5, 138, 190
    see also anxiety; depression; stress
migration, 184
Milne, A.A., 162

mind, and body, 101–3
mission statements, 43
Mitchell, Wendy, 217, 225–6
Monbiot, George, 163
money, 89, 169–78, 205
muscle memory, 111

NASA, 137–8
neighbours, 69, 161–6, 182–3
neoliberalism, 185
Neustatter, Angela, 73, 154
night classes, 69, 160
nuclear proliferation, 185

Obama, Barack, 185–6
Obama, Michelle, 29
obesity, 98
obituaries, 25–6
O'Donohue, John, 12, 209
O'Farrell, Maggie, 238
O'Gorman, Patrick, 230
olive oil, 98–9
online dating, 69
optimism, 34, 43
Ó Tuama, Pádraig, 168, 208
Owen, James P, 97

Palahniuk, Chuck, 146
Paltrow, Gwyneth, 126
parents, 74–80
peace, 186–7
pensions, 4, 169, 172, 175, 186
Phillips, Adam, 32

planning, 199–206
    and assets, 203–4
play, 134–45
Pooley, Arthur, 46
population growth, 184
problem ownership, 80
property investments, 171–2
proverbs, 64, 72, 114
Public Health England, 92
purpose, 30, 40–53
    and anaesthetics, 44–5
    and neglect, 50

Rantzen, Dame Esther, 67
recycling, 15, 56, 181, 188
relationships, 30, 64–88, 107–8
    and death, 242, 257
    maintaining, 73
    and money, 177
    pause button, 87
    see also parents; siblings
religion and spirituality, 69, 109,
    261–2
retirement villages, 150–2
Richards, Keith, 172
Roberts, Rhian, 222
Rohr, Richard, 41
Rowe, Cecil, 141
running, 37, 39, 93–4
Saul, Peter, 237
saying sorry, 81
Schrader, Paul, 120
Schwartz, Barry, 178

298 | Index

Scorsese, martin, 120
Scott, Andrew, 136, 199
scrambled-egg brain, 5
sex, 81
Shaw, George Bernard, 134
Sherman, James R., 1, 267
shopping, 43
siblings, 78–80, 175–6
silence, 84
Silver Line, 67, 186, 276
Simpson, Homer, 241
sleep, 109–13
Sleeping Beauty, 238
Sliding Doors, 126
Slimming World, 99
Smith, Harry Leslie, 184–5
Smith-Stanley, Edward, 91
smoking, 107, 109, 112
Social Relationships and Mortality Risk, 164
Socrates, 258
soul, 41
Southall, Neville, 128
Street Child World Cup, 238
stress, 105–7
stroke, 92, 99
Stuart, Mags, 51–2
sugar, 99
suicide, 237
Sullivan, Harry Stack, 210
supper clubs, 189–90

Tale of Peter Rabbit, The, 238

Taxi Driver, 120
technology
    advances in, 183–4, 186
    wearable, 96–8
TED Talks, 48, 66
tennis, 211
terminal patients, 24–6
Thomas, Amelia, 69, 262
Thurman, Howard, 206
transition, 227–35
travel opportunities, 186–7
trees, 13–15, 115–16
Trump, Donald, 179
trust, 65, 70, 73, 82, 158, 162, 168, 230
Turner, Steve, 86
Tversky, Amos, 212
Twain, Mark, 145

values, 30, 54–63, 177
    collapse of societal morals, 184
    and death, 242, 256
Vincent, Professor Richard, 89–90, 181, 245
vitamins, 100
vulnerability, 32, 44, 64, 70, 160

Waldinger, Professor Robert, 66, 137
walking, 37, 39, 46, 69, 91–4, 134, 138, 188, 220
Ware, Bronnie, 24
wearable technology, 96–8

Webster, Isobel, 128, 130–1, 250
Welsh, Irvine, 44
widows and widowers, 260–1
Wilde, Oscar, 43
Wilkes, Sam, 216
wills, 249–50, 257
Wilson, Pip, 35
Wise, Greg, 241–2
work, 117–33

world, the, 179–92
World Health Organization, 90, 111
Wroe, Martin, 245, 255, 260

Unbound is the world's first crowdfunding publisher, established in 2011.

We believe that wonderful things can happen when you clear a path for people who share a passion. That's why we've built a platform that brings together readers and authors to crowdfund books they believe in – and give fresh ideas that don't fit the traditional mould the chance they deserve.

This book is in your hands because readers made it possible. Everyone who pledged their support is listed below. Join them by visiting unbound.com and supporting a book today.

Antonio Cantafio

Caring4Elders www.
    caring4eldersuk.co.uk

Bekki Clark

Jonathan Cole

Penny Coulthard

John Crawford

Liz Curran

Tricia Cusden

Shôn Dale-Jones

Stephen Davies

Sally Davis

Gillian Delaney

Claire Diedrichsen

Glenn Dietz

Malcolm Doney

Suzanne Doyle-Morris

S. R. Dreamholde

Gary Duckworth

Caroline Duffy

Julia Duncan

Valerie Dunsford

EQ Investors

David Farrer

Rosie Faunch

Chris & Anne Fendick

Glyn Fussell

Richard Germain

Joanna Glass

Adrian Goodall

Mark Goodier

Annette Greenhalgh

Cathy Griffiths

Simon Gunn

Nick Hadley

Chris Hall

Georgina Hall

Elaine Halligan

Janine Hamilton

Irene M Hannah

Andy & Sibylle Harrison

Tim and Jane Hawkes

Claire Heald

Abi Hewitt

Garth and Gill Hewitt

The Hewson Family

Sheila Higgins

Felicity Higginson

Emma Hodgson

Deborah Hofman

Jeanie Honey

J Howey

Harold Hoyle

Natasha and Daniel Hulls

Lesley Hunt

Nicholas Ibery

Helen Idle

Robert Iles

Andrew Ingram

David Jenkins

Joanne Jenkins

Laurel Johnson

Phil Johnstone

Graham Judd

Craig Keeler-Milne

Mark Kenner

Jane Kershaw

Ed Kessler

Dan Kieran

Jeremy King

David Kirkup

Deborah Larsson

Angela Law

Chris Law

Kim Lee-Own

Claire Lewis

Penny Lewis

Nikki Livingstone-Rothwell

Jane Lockie

Seonaid Mackenzie

Susan Mactavish

Michael Marks

H & S Mayo

Hannah Mayo

Kate McCorquodale

Kevin McCullough

Stephen McGoldrick

Annette Mercer

John Mitchinson

Alison Moffatt

Kevin Moran

Joerg Mueller-Kindt

Ellen Myrup

Nicky Napier

Antonella Napolitano

Josephine Nash

Steve Nation

Carlo Navato

Helen Needham

Andrew Neligan (Retirement
    Planner)

Lasse Nielsen

Liz Norris

Dean O'Connor

Christine Olaitan Shoruna

Neil Palmer

Nicky Parkinson

Peter Parsons

Emma Pearce

Michelle Pearson

John Perkins

Dorothy Peyton Jones

Ralf Pflugfelder

Angie Phillips

Justin Pollard

Marijke Powis

Julian Price

Susan Quilliam

Ruth and Graham Raw

Adam Reid

Angela Reith

Matilda Reith

Rosie Reith

Phoebe Reith Ibery

Aprille Rigby

Richard Robbins

Sarah Rose

Beverley Sage

R D Sansom

Rob Saunders

Vera Schuster Beesley

Joe Schwan

Jenny Scott
Liz Scott
The Scott family
Fi Segel
Brian Sibley
Mary Steel
Craig Stobo
Emma Supple
Ian Sutcliffe
Alex Tarry
Jochen Theis
Lesley Thompson
Mary Thompson
Padraig O Tuama
Ann Tyler
Ralph Van Dijk
Elie Vanvlasselaer
Craig Vaughton

Richard Vincent
André Vögtlin
Catherine Walker
Janet Walker
Isobel Webster
Anita Whitehead
Donie Wiley
Dean & Emma Willars
Enid Williams
Willie Williams
Caroline Wilson
Ed Wolf
Wendy Wood
Joanne Wroe
Martin Wroe
Julie Wych
Eleanor Youdell